EMERSON EDITION

presents

a

Howard Burnham and Richard Butterworth
production

GRONES

DICTIONARY OF

MUSIC

or

A GOLDEN TREASURY OF
MUSICAL RUBBISH

or

MISLEADING LIVES OF THE
GREAT COMPOSERS

—

Dedicated, anyway, to the
Ampleforth Colliery Band

Now read on . . .

Emerson Edition, Windmill Farm, Ampleforth, Yorkshire, England.

First published 1978

© Emerson Edition, 1978.

Set and printed in Theme by De Mandus Print Ltd.,
29 - 31 Union Street, High Barnet, Hertfordshire.

All rights reserved. This book is sold subject to the conditions that it shall not, by way of trade or otherwise, be lent, re-sold, hired out, or otherwise circulated without the publisher's prior consent in any form of binding or cover other than that in which it is published and without a similar condition including this condition being imposed on the subsequent purchaser.

ISBN 0 9506209 0 4

GRONE'S DICTIONARY OF MUSIC

Contents

Foreword by Fritz Spiegl	6
ANON (Circa)	7
B.A.C.H.	9
BEETHOVEN, Ludwig van	11
BERLIOZ, Louis Hector	13
BRAHMS, Johannes	15
A NESTE OF SINGING BYRDS	17
CHOPIN, Fryderyk Franciszek	19
A CZECH LIST	21
THE DAME, THE KNIGHT & THE ENIGMA	23
DEBUSSY, Claude Achille	25
GRIEG, Edvard Hagerup	27
HANDEL, George Frideric	29
HAYDN, Franz Joseph	31
HOLST, R.V.W.	33
LISZT, Ferenc	35
LULLY, Jean Baptiste	37
MAHLER, Anton	38
BRUCKNER, Gustav	41
MENDELSSOHN, Jacob Ludwig Felix	43
MOZART, Joannes Chrysostomus Wolfgangus Theophilus (= Gottlieb = Amadeus)	45
PUCCINI, Giacomo Antonio Domenico Michele Secondo Maria	47
PURCELL, Henry	49
ROSSINI, Gioacchino Antonio	51
RUSSIAN EMIGRES, the	53
SCHOENBERG, Arnold	55
SCHUBERT, Franz Peter	57
SCHUMANN, Robert Alexander	59
SOUSA, John Philip	61
STRAUSS, the compleat	63
STRAVINSKY, Igor	65
SULLIVAN, Sir William Seymour Schwenk	67
TCHAIKOVSKY, Pyotr Ilyich	69
VERDI, Giuseppe	71
VIVALDI, Antonio	73
WAGNER, Wilhelm Richard	75
WEBER, Carl Maria Friedrich Ernst von	77
MODERN, er, MUSIC	79
INDEX	81
THE AUTHORS	85

FOREWORD
by Fritz Spiegl

To the Reader:

Being funny about music is extremely difficult nowadays. Advertise a humorous concert and your audience, if you get one, will sit there with clenched teeth and mutter, 'Right then, make me laugh. If you can.' It was easy at one time. We used to do it regularly in Liverpool, inventing April Fools Concerts. Then along came Gerard Hoffnung (who started his career as a professional musical funny man after being invited to perform at one of our AFCs in 1955 or 6) and, egged on by his agents and publishers, turned it into an industry. After that came the avant garde. (And 'It's hard/for the avant-garde/for this year's art nouveau/becomes next year's vieux chapeau'). They filled their pianos with nuts, made it up as they went along, twiddled electrics, made rude noises — all of which we'd been doing for years — but now no-one laughed. They weren't meant to. Not even the performers, except when they got their pay packets.

Thus the bottom dropped out of funny music. Parody killed with self-parody.

It's even harder to write a funny foreword to a genuinely funny book about music. But as with most humorists, the authors' underlying purpose is deeply serious. There are few crazy facts in this book which, when investigated, don't turn out to have some basis of truth.

That's why I found it very funny, in the privacy of my own home.

July 1978

*love from
Fritz*

ANON — (Circa)

Anon (circa) was an extremely prolific and active composer, bird-fancier and member of the regular clergy. Of astounding virtuosity and capacity, he was quite capable of singing in the Lydian, Aeolian, Hypomixolydian and Dorian Grayian modes whilst simultaneously enjoying a Benedictine, a Chartreuse and a Grand Marnier, thereby establishing the link between the muse and the muscatel so stoutly maintained in our own day by the £.$.Q. (if Private Eye is to be believed).

In the course of a long life -- he kept an illuminated missal in the attic — he wrote extensively for the rebec, vielle, cornetto, shawm-off sackbut (as used by robber barons), regal, pommer, crumhorn, tea-cake and muffin. He provided the musical backing for the Hundred Years War and the Black Death — in the latter processions of penitents happily beat one another with flageolets.

By about A.D. 800 Anon had become a bird fancier, keeping and breeding a team of racing parrots who were actually cleverly disguised pigeons, (hence the name polyphony). These intelligent birds were trained to sing in several parts (polyglots) with a portative organ filling in the bass line (polyfilla). Alas, these wings of song were clipped by the Council of Trent and the parrots left the monasteries at the Reformation (polygon).

Anon tried the same thing with cuckoos, but found them unresponsively duotonous. Nevertheless, his hit number 'Sumer is icumen in' was a product of this experimental period. Anon died (?) in an odour of sanctity under a monastery dovecote during the 14th, 15th or 16th century. Attempts by frustrated musicologists to attribute the works of Anon to Pope Gregory, Henry VIII or even Shakespeare are to be resisted. It is also quite untrue that Anon was a woman, although she may once have been a choirboy.

JOHANN SEBASTIAN BACH
(1685 - 1750)

Bach (B.A.C.H.), the marathon parent and long distance walker, was born in 1685 at Eisenach, which was already famous as the home of four generations of musicians called Bach. Young Bach, in order to distinguish himself from all the other Bachs (B.A.C.H.S.), called himself Johann Sebastian and trained as a marathon walker (Hamburg, 60 miles, Lubeck, 200 miles). But the prizes were so meagre — two herring heads and a few free tickets to organ recitals — that he took up composition instead.

He became Kapellmeister to various princely families, composing the six well-known concertos for the now forgotten instrument, the brandenburg, and the set of 'Goldberg' or 'Ovaltine' variations for insomniac and harpsichord. Although he was not a romantic composer, Bach married twice. His first wife was the 'stranger maiden' whom he compromised in the Arnstadt organ loft whilst working on a two part fantasia; and his second wife was the very popular and accommodating Anna Magdalenabuch, whom everyone tries.

Always a devout anglican, Bach became organist and choirmaster at Cantorbury Cathedral, Leipzig (sometimes erroneously called St. Thomas's Church after the martyred archbishop). Here Bach was famous for his furious rages ('Passions'), and his irascibility with inattentive choirboys was legendary. 'The Genghis Khan of the choir stalls', he wigged them constantly and even tenors and basses quailed before the new Khan Tartar.

Bach is sometimes called 'the Father of Music' because he had twenty sons and daughters as well as forty-eight preludes and fugues. He died, overcome by his labours, in 1750. Many of his sons became celebrated B.A.C.H.S. too; Wilhelm Friedemann (known as 'Wilf' Bach), the twins G.C.E. and C.S.E. Bach (the latter a celebrated modal composer) and Johann Christian, the so-called 'English Bach' (B.A.R.K.). Finally it is rumoured that there was even a Welsh one (Die Eisteddfod Bach.)

LUDWIG VAN BEETHOVEN
(1770 - 1827)

Beethoven received his musical training earlier than any other great composer. At approximately two o'clock every morning, his father, a failed singer but a highly successful drunkard, would lurch home and pull little Ludwig from bed for some five finger exercises. Vater Beethoven's baby-bashing tactics worked, for by the time Lugwig was twelve he was harpsichordist to the Eau de Cologne (to whom he was later to dedicate his Symphony No. 5, the "Chanel"). His perfumed patron sent the young musician to Vienna to study harmony, counterpoint and personality clash with 'Papa' Haydn.

The headstrong youth regarded his teacher as a tonal totalitarian, and antagonised the old man by calling him ' Uncle Joe '. Unruly and passionate, Beethoven gave unruly and appassionata piano lessons to aristocratic young ladies, and became abusive when their fathers showed him the door. One of the founders of the Ramblers' Association, he wrote much of his music on invigorating hikes through brooks during passing thunder storms 'mit die knapsack on die back'.

He was a fervent admirer of Napoleon and dedicated his 3rd Symphony to the great French revolutionary leader. It is well known that, when Napoleon made himself Emperor, Beethoven erased his name from the title page and furiously turned him into a piano concerto. His one great opera, 'Fidelio', sometimes known as ' Jail House Rocco ', has four overtures, three of whom are confusingly called 'Leonore'. In this opera, Beethoven was accused of taking the pizarro out of the status quo.

From about the age of thirty onwards Beethoven experimented with ear trumpets, but never completed a successful concerto for them. However, he did write the famous set of string quartets for Court Orlovsky's Viennese Pink Champagne parties. In his declining years Beethoven became increasingly violent and indulged in piano-smashing competitions, writing the 'Hammerklavier Sonata' for one such. It is not surprising, then, that English admirers, fearing for his sanity, sent him a Broadmoor piano.

His last great symphony, described by many critics as a mind-blowing experience, was indeed the world's first drug culture composition which explains why it is called the 'Chloral'. He died in yet another passing thunder storm, the lightning striking an ear-trumpet with which he was conducting at the time.

HECTOR BERLIOZ
(1803 - 1869)

Hector Berlioz, the Royal Hunt jockey and boot fetishist, was born near Grenoble, where he early developed alarming enthusiasms for pink boots, the guitar and Virgil. In the former passion, he ardently pursued a young lady called Stella who sported a magnificent pair. His father, deeply concerned, sent him to Paris to dissect corpses in the city morgue as the only possible cure. But Hector cut dissecting and joined the cast of the original 'Vie de Bohème', earning a great reputation for Cherubinibaiting (a popular 19th century Romantic pastime).

He then became interested in the turf and entered five times for the coveted Prix de Rome, finally winning it in 1830 with a blazing run on a colt called Sardanapalus. Meanwhile he had discovered that Shakespeare was a woman called Harriet Smithson, and he asked her to marry him with the help of a large orchestra and a set of fantastic tubular bells.

Hector, under the assumed name of Harold, travelled in Italy, where he upset the locals by rolling in ecstasy on the banks of the Arno with Sir Walter Scott and Shakespeare. He was asked to leave. Back in Paris he infuriated the music critics by writing better criticism than they, and by pulling the wool over their ears, with his 'Shepherds' Farewell' chorus (Gold Medal, Alsace Sheep Dog Trials, 1854).

He wrote his 'Song of the Railwaymen' to a commission from the Caledonian Steam Locomotion Company, which explains why it is sometimes known as the 'Waverley Station Overture'. Berlioz scandalised polite society with his bad language and anticlericalism, even going so far as to write an opera called 'The Bloody Nun' (Papal Index, 1847).

His masterpiece 'The Trojans' was badly received on account of its hectoring tone. Berlioz travelled extensively but always returned to what he called his 'idée fixe' — pink boots. In the late 1860s he returned to his birthplace, seeking the original Stella of roseate footwear fame, only to die in disillusion on discovering that she now wore black patent leather ones.

YOUR HIGHNESS BRAHMS
(1833 - 1897)

Brahms, the 'hot dog' of late German Romanticism, was a Hamburger, and proud of it. His father was an impoverished double bass player, who scraped feverishly together enough thalers to advance his son's talents in piano lessons from Edward 'Chico' Marxsen. The boy gave his first recitals 'dusting the ivories' in low Bierkellers, which he would enter with his legendary remark, "I ham only hier for ze bier, bitte."

The gifted lad was stolen by the gypsies to be the accompanist of the celebrated Romany fiddler, Reményi. The two musicians trudged the highways and byways, living in the hedgerows and on the hedgehogs, until Brahms was rescued by the great violinist Joachim. Almost overnight Brahms' fortunes changed. The gauche, uncouth and extremely rude youth rapidly became a gauche, uncouth and unbelievably rude great composer.

He got off to a flying start by snoring through a performance of Liszt's B minor Sonata given by the composer, and later went on to score several direct hits on Wagner, Bruckner, Hugo Wolf, all the French composers and Cambridge University, whose honorary doctorate he snubbed. (They replied by giving him the Bruch off).

He was adopted by Frau Schumann who maternally attempted to give him some polish, but he never took to the polonaise. In 1856 he was appointed musical director to the Duke (sometimes rendered 'Prince') of Detmold, for whose late wife Brahms composed the celebrated 'Duchess Requiem'. A deeply romantic yet solitary man, Brahms made several tragic overtures to young ladies, but fortunately nothing came of them, and their interest is only academic.

The last years of his life were spent in Vienna, where, because of his pre-eminence, people would address him as 'Your Highness' Brahms, which infuriated Wagner measure beyond measure. He was a great favourite with the children because of his amazing resemblance to Santa Claus, whose variations (wrongly attributed to St. Anthony) he had composed. In 1897 he attended the funeral of Frau Schumann, writing the 'Four Serious Songs' including 'Gaudeamus Igitur', but caught a chill himself and died soon after.

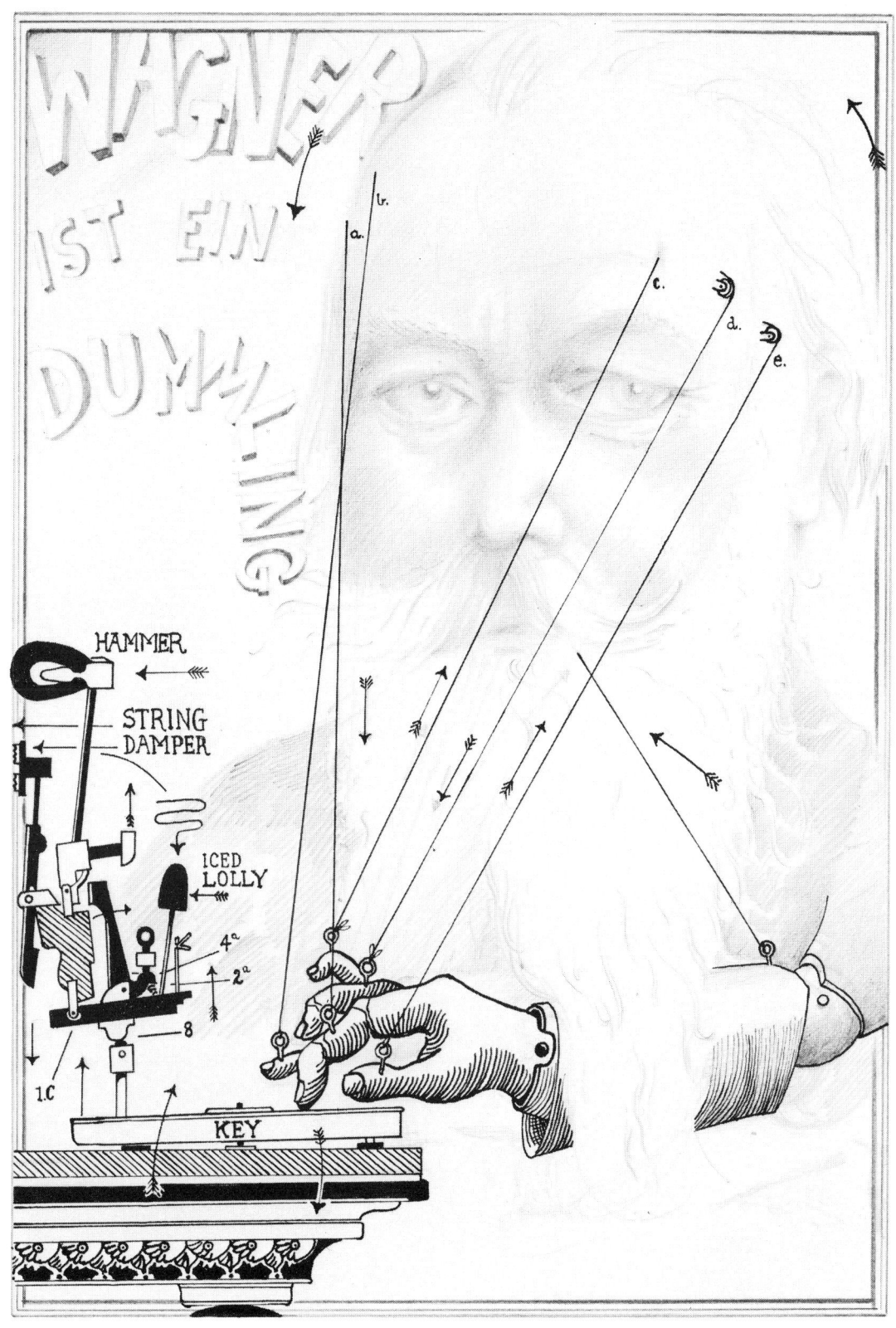

A NESTE OF SINGING BYRDS
(Active 1550 - 1620)

It is truly said that 'byrds of a feather flocke together', and certainly they did in the Merrie (non-German) England of Bluff Queen Bess. This was the Golden Age of English Music when potatoes were in their infancy but poetasters were in their prime. The Forest of Arden was full of full-throated farthingales, their quills a-quiver to snatch a bawdy catch, usually about cuckoos. The 'byrds' would meet at their taverner to down a stoup of canary and, with their strumpets, run over the latest coranto (this was known as 'a night on the viols').

And what a dazzling galaxy of talent was there! Shakespeare (known as the Silver Swan of Avon), Kit Marlowe (liable to be galliarded in the gizzard at any moment), Ben Jonson (drinking not only with his eyes, but with his mouth, ears and nose as well), and these were only the lyricists. Among the great composers were Giles 'Dozy' Farnaby, Johnny 'Cry Baby' Dowland, Doctor John Bovril, Orlando the Marmalade Monkey, Old Uncle Tom Tallis and all.

It is often overlooked that the most famous instrumentalist of the period was in fact Francis Drake, the celebrated Devonshire drummer. His percussive effects in the Armada (Caprice Espagnol) are legendary, and his performances on the metallic dulcimer earned him the nickname of 'Toledo Blades of the Spanish Main'. It is interesting to note that he earned his fame despite a tendency to drop off during 500 bar rests — "Captain, art thou sleeping there below?" — and he was indeed the first musician to be knighted for his services to music. This happened after the first performance of his great round called 'Circumnavigation'.

Patroness of such remarkable talent was Bluff Queen Bess, herself a talented musician and known as the Virginal Queen for her triumphs on the Ocarina. This instrument, sometimes known as the sweet potato, had just been introduced to England by 'Spud' Raleigh. It is sometimes said that Queen Elizabeth was a man. Certainly she may have been an usurper, for musicologists have proved that England's rightful ruler, Victoria, was living and working in Spanish exile at the time (composing a set of Spanish octets known as 'pieces of eight'). And if Elizabeth was a man, then Shakespeare, *ipso facto*, was a woman. *(Vide* Berlioz *supra).*

FRYDERYK CHOPIN
(1810 - 1849)

The original French polisher of the piano, Fryderyk Franciszek Chopin was born near Warsaw where his father reputedly gave French lessons to young aristocratic ladies. His mother was herself a déclassée aristo but not as déclassée as all that, for little Fryd hobnobbed with the Czartoryskis and Radziwitts (though not the Kennedys). Of extraordinary delicate beauty with an aureole of auburn hair, Chopin was never a choirboy. Instead his sensitive alabaster fingers caressed the keyboards and heartstrings of maternal Polish noblewomen who fed him pastilles and recommended brands of linctus for that nasty cough that was troubling him.

In his adolescence he became a keen Polish nationalist or national pollster. Here the opinion was that he should travel before the ruling Russian secret police persuaded him to continue his studies in Siberia. Arriving in the Paris of 1831, Frédéric François Chopin (as he francostyled himself) pleyel-ed around on various pianos with Liszt, Thalberg, Herz of piano-rental fame, Czerny and "Whoops I'm a" Pixis in a protracted mathematical contest set by Bellini called the 'Hexameron'. Cherubini was unimpressed, but he was an old set square anyway.

A keen amateur ornithologist, Chopin did some very successful nocturnal field studies. He also became music master to several aristocratic young French noblewomen. He enjoyed moving in wealthy circles though it made him feverishly giddy. He was antipathetic to 'La Vie de Bohème', perhaps because he knew too much about Mimi's cough.

In 1837 he first met George Sand, the Sally Bowles of the Boulevards (or 19th century thinking man's crumpet), who mothered him and ravished him by turns. Overwhelmed he made two dreary visits to England. On one of these he played before Queen Victoria at the Duchess of Sutherland's, but argylessly omitted to play any Mendlessohn. The Queen was not amused and poor Chopin did not receive a bartholdy.

He returned to Paris unable to get it off his chest, and all too soon it was time for the B^b minor slow movement into Père Lachaise. The lad from Warsaw had written two piano concertos as well as the celluloid 'Warsaw Concerto' whose remarkable anticipation of Rakhmaninov gives it an added sell.

A CZECH LIST

From Bohemia's woods and fields has come a strongly nationalistic school of composers, started originally by Good King Wenceslas, who praguematically built the Cathedral of St. Vitus, the patron saint of ballet. His work was continued by Jan Hus, who insisted that composing should be done in the vernacular. Unhappily, the Moravians wanted it in Moravian, whilst the Slavs wanted it in Slav and the Church wanted it in Latin. So Hus was burned at the stake, obtained from nearby Transylvania.

The next major figure in the history of Czech music is the celebrated 17th century organist Andreas Hammerschmidt, known as 'the Flyover' for his skilful fingerwork. The 18th century was dominated by the Stamitz family who gleefully wrote each other's music and told interlopers to mannheim their own business.

Czech nationalism came into its own, just like every other brand, in the 19th century. Bedřich Smetana led the way in Czech music, despite the rumour that he sold it down the Moldau. The cheerful son of a brewer, he grew up into a genial dog-loving, pipe-smoking, wife-beating man ('The Battered Bride'). He also beat Harrison Birtwistle. This was done by becoming the first musical director of a National Theatre, over a hundred years before our own Punch and Judy man.

His reputation suffered a decline as a result of the publication of his highly compromising intimate letters, after which he ruefully wrote the six symphonic poems called 'Blast'. He was given a flea in his ear, sometimes mistranslated as a persistent high E.

The other leading figure of the Czech national school was Antonín Dvořák, the celebrated loco-spotter and innumerate. In his youth he was the whistling butcher's boy from Prague who did humouresque things with strings of sausages. He is remembered for his trip to the USA, where Yale students for a rag joke circulated the rumour that the 'New World Symphony' was written by Scott Joplin.

It is often forgotten that he spent many happy hours of his American visit among the rolling stock at Grand Central Station. However he missed Pacific 231. Dvořák is also celebrated as the most inept mathematician in music. He had no concept of numerical progression whatsoever. Thus Symphony No.3 is really No. 5, No. 1 is No. 6, No. 2 is No. 7, No. 4 is No. 8, No. 5 is No. 9 and vice versa, except for Opus 76 which is really Opus 24. Not surprisingly, music publishers nicknamed him ' Dumky '.

His daughter married the famous Japanese composer Suk, who is remembered for his symphonic study of a Kamikaze pilot, 'The Angel of Death'. Our Czech list ends appropriately with Leoš Janáček, who put an end to Hus's 500-year-old vernacular controversy by doing it in Glagolitic.

THE DAME, THE KNIGHT & THE ENIGMA
(1857 - 1944)

Many critics and musicologists have vainly attempted to solve the puzzle of Elgar's 'Enigma Variations'. The solution lies not in the music but in the title, the first and last letters of which form the initials ' E.S. ' for Ethel Smyth. When it is consequently realised that Ethel Smyth was in fact Edward Elgar in drag, the sauce of the Worcester composer becomes apparent.

Elgar had spent his formative years, according to Professor K. Russell, as a keen member of the Pony Club thundering over the Malvern Hills whilst simultaneously composing the 'Introduction and Allegro'. It was his marriage to a general's daughter in 1889 that gave him the idea of his travesty persona of ' Ethel Smyth ', a general's daughter.

Fortunately his wife Alice was very understanding. His daring transvestite debut was given before Queen Victoria and the Empress Eugénie at Osborne. On this occasion he performed 'Ethel's' Mass in falsetto and a pair of falsies (which he jokingly called 'The Bosom's Mate'). The august ladies were completely fooled, though it is rumoured that John Brown rumbled him in highly embarrassing circumstances but was too drunk to remember it next morning.

Not long after this Elgar was arrested outside 221b Baker Street as the most notorious cocaine pusher in London Town, but cleverly effected a sex change in the cells at Bow Street and joined a group of militant suffragettes bound for Holloway. Here he wrote his great votes-for-women opera 'The Wreckers' about the redoubtable band of suffragettes who smashed the windows of Whitehall. The Lord Chamberlain's Office subsequently turned into a Cornish pasty.

In old age Edward/Ethel became a keen dog-lover, who expressly wrote 'The Starlight Barking' (to a libretto by Dodie Smyth) and the 'Pomeranian and Circumstance Marches' for the Three Crufts Festivals. With unerring audaciousness he secured a knighthood for himself and a damehood for his other self, the first great dame ever to win at Cruft's.

ACHILLE CLAUDE DEBUSSY
(1862 - 1918)

Debussy, the iconoclast of musical convention, was born in his parents' china shop in St. Germain-en-Laye. He studied the piano with Madame de Fleurville, celebrated as the mother of Verlaine's wife and consequently the butt of Rimbaud's worst mother-in-law jokes. Little Claude entered the Conservatoire at the precocious age of eleven. A delicate child, he took a penta tonic which wholly toned him up, though it infuriated his professors.

At the age of eighteen, he was collected by Madame von Meck for her musical menagerie and taken to Russia, but he escaped and returned to Paris. Celebrated as the 'enfant terrible' of the Conservatoire, he won the Rome Prize with a cantata diplomatically entitled 'L'Enfant Prodigue'. He detested life at the Villa d'Este and returned after only two years to make the exciting discovery of Gamelan, his beautiful green-eyed idol from Java, with whom he co-habited for several years. He called her ' Gamy ' for short.

At the Exposition Universelle of 1889, he was unimpressed by the Eiffel Tower, but the works of Monet, Degas, Renoir and Cézanne made a lasting impression on him and his music. About this time he wrote an unravelled string quartet for the famous Belgian violinist, Eyore, and the celebrated symphonic poem, 'Afternoon of an Ibex'.

Like many fin-de-siècle aesthetes, he became obsessed with Maeterlinck's great symbolist romance 'Pelléas at Mélisande' or 'Love on Great Dole'. With the poet's permission, Debussy turned the play into his celebrated opera known as 'Gollaudwog's Cake Walk', in which the doomed lovers fêteful romance is subtly treated with every nuance and nuage. Rehearsals were stormy, for Maeterlinck wanted his wife to sing Mélisande, and Debussy's choice, the young Scottish soprano, Mary Garden, was often in tears. The composer charmingly wrote ' Jardin dans la Pluie' to console her.

His first marriage, to Rosalie Texier ('La Demoiselle Elue') was not blessed, but his liason with the ' Merry Widow ' Emma Bardac was. She gave him his only child, a daughter, curiously named ' Cabbage '. After protracted divorce proceedings, Debussy was able to marry Emma, and he saluted her as the mother of his child with the symphonic sketches 'La Mère'.

At the outbreak of the Great War, Debussy indulged in some virulent Boche-baiting in his 'Monsieur Croche' articles which violently castigated German music. A formidable female Teuton critic called Bertha Krupp replied, and under 'Big Bertha's' bombardment Debussy expired.

EDVARD GRIEG
(1843 - 1907)

Like the 'Skye Boat Song' and 'Drambuie', Edvard Grieg forms a celebrated link with the '45. His ancestor, Alexander Greig of Aberdeen, skirled his sporran for the Bonnie Prince and was advised to take a prolonged Scandinavian holiday after Culloden. The Griegs, as they now called themselves, intermarried with the impeccably Nordic Hagerups, and the eventual result was wee Edvard Hagerup Grieg, the world's first Scottish-Norwegian midget.

His mother taught him the piano as soon as he could reach the keys, which wasn't very early. His potential as a composer was first picked out by the famous Norwegian violinist and picador, Ole Bull, who persuaded his parents to let little Edvard study at Leipzig. It was not a great success. The professors paid little attention to him because they never saw him: he was so tiny that he was scarcely visible behind a piano.

He travelled to Copenhagen where he met Rikard Nordraak, who introduced him to the trolls and he never looked back. He also met the amazingly ugly dramatist, Henrik Ibsen, for whom he rather tactlessly wrote 'The Queer Squint Music'. Grieg later travelled to Weimar where he showed his famous A minor Piano Concerto to the great Ferenc Liszt, who was so excited by the cadenza modulation that he coined the phrase "Gee! that's great!"

Returning to Norway, Grieg married his cousin Nina Hagerup, who was a gifted singer and fortunately also a midget. Together they gave recitals, barely visible above the potted plants fronting the stage. Grieg, a virtuoso pianist, was continually encouraged by the great Liszt, and as a token of gratitude Grieg wrote a choral work, 'At the Gates of a Southern Cloister' for Liszt's Abbey *(vide* Liszt *infra)*.

Now a pensioner of the Norwegian Government, Grieg could afford to build his picturesque retreat for composition and practice called 'Troldhaugen' ('The Hall of the Trill King'). Here, as he became increasingly famous, flocks of tourists came to see the celebrated Grieg gnomes in their natural environment. Owing to ill-health he wrote few large scale works, but he was a perfect miniaturist. His music has been accused of unadventurous lyricism, but it is often forgotten that he was a pioneer of twelve-tone composition. After all, he wrote the lyrical whole Berg Suite.

GEORGE FRIDERIC HANDEL (1685 - 1759)

Handel was born Georg Friederich Händel (or Haendel) in the little German town of Halle, which he was later to immortalise in his 'Hallelujah Chorus'. He was known locally as 'that little bleeder Händel' because he often helped his father, a barber-surgeon, with the leeches. His father hoped that little Georg would enter the legal profession and was most upset when the little sucker stuck to music with leech-like tenacity.

Young Händel (or Haendel) taught himself to play the bones (or clavicle), and the story is often told of how he kept the skeleton in the attic for secret practice. He studied opera and fencing with Johann Mattheson in Hamburg, where their gem-like performances on the sharpsichord were known as the 'Clown Duels'.

Händel (or Haendel) travelled to Italy and there changed his name to Giorgio Frederico Händel, and made the acquaintance of the celebrated Spanish-Irish composer Scarlatti O'Habanera. Returning to Germany, he was appointed Kapellmeister to the Ejector of Hanover, but Händel soon threw him over and travelled to England, where, being a German composer, he naturally wrote a series of popular Italian operas.

He became famous for his good living, the malicious remarking that his nose was often 'ruddier than the cherry,' the result of copious infusions of Händel's lager. For a time he worked for the Duke of Chandos at the ducal estate of Cannons, but was eventually fired.

In 1714, the Ejector of Hanover took his seat on the English throne as King George I, and it was rumoured that relations with his former Kapellmeister were somewhat stormy, but Handel poured oil on troubled water with his celebrated 'Grease Music'. At about this time, he rescored his name as George Frideric Handel without the double dotting. He became a pasteurised Englishman and composed many oratorios which went down a treat with his conservative English patrons. (It is significant that he wrote no orawhigios).

He composed the 'Royal Fireworks Music' for the peace of Aix-la-Chapelle, which went off with a premature bang, drowning the music and precipitating the Seven Years' War.

In his old age he was afflicted by blindness, but Eric Fenby generously acted as amanuensis, working on the second version of the 'Oil on Water Music', known as 'Summer Night on the River'. The aged composer eventually died of frustration and apoplexy when his royal patron refused to give him a handle to his name in the honours list.

JOSEPH HAYDN
(1732 - 1809)

Haydn, music's Till Eulenspiegel (until Richard Strauss), was born on All Fools' Day and early developed into a talented merry prankster. His father was celebrated as the only harp-playing cartwheel manufacturer in Rohrau, where his devotion to serious music earned him the nickname of the 'square wheelwright'. His son, Joseph, had a good ear, a pleasing voice and lovely fair hair, so he was sent to Vienna to be a choirboy. But here his high spirits got him into considerable trouble, like the time he startled the Empress Maria Theresa with his celebrated gorilla impersonation. She ordered the 'impudent monkey' to be flogged. On another famous occasion when his voice was breaking the Empress cruelly remarked, "He sounds like a crowing rooster." Ever the joker, Haydn dedicated his 'Hen Symphony' to her.

The story is often told of his dismissal for cutting a 'pigtail' off a fellow chorister. In fact, the crime was more serious, and the unfortunate victim of the outrage sang castrato for the rest of his days. Fortunately, the dismissed Haydn was soon taken into the service of the aristocratic Esterantzen family, and worked for thirty years at their fog-bound palace of Esterház, where Prince Nikolaus was the possessor of a fine baryton voice. In close harmony with his musical patron, it was here that Haydn composed many of his eighty-three barber shop quartets.

Also at Esterház he wrote the two concertos for foghorn and the well-known 'Farewell Symphony'. This latter work was written to remind his patron that one day there would be something called the Musicians' Union. Unfortunately, the Prince and his guests, full of a good dinner, were fast asleep by the last movement, and the effect went for nothing. Haydn, ever the resilient joker, replied with the 'Surprise Symphony', which caused the Prince a mild seizure and nearly cost Haydn his job. (This is sometimes called a 'London Symphony', but everyone knows Vaughan Williams wrote that.)

The composer made an unfortunate marriage to the termagant daughter of a wig-maker. She had no liking for music, and used Haydn's manuscripts for curl-papers remarking tartly, "My mother bids me bind my hair!" She created constantly and Haydn dedicated 'The Representation of Chaos' to her. They separated soon after.

In 1799 Haydn composed his celebrated 'Nelson or "Hello Sailor!" Mass' to honour the visit to Esterház of the famous English admiral after his victory at the Nile. Nelson was so pleased that he uttered the immortal words, "Kiss me, Haydn!" In 1809, as the Emperor Napoleon's French army was besieging Vienna, Haydn cautiously composed 'The Emperor's Hymn' to welcome the conqueror. Fortunately for his reputation he died and kind friends quickly changed the title to 'Austria'. *(Hymns Ancient & Modern, nos 292 and 545!).*

R.V.W. HOLST — English Country Gardener (1872 - 1958)

Just before the Great War an army of earnest young musicians wearing combat knickerbockers and equipped only with bicycles and Edison-Bell recording machines terrorised the villages of rural England and America, waylaying unsuspecting ancients, plying them with drink and then ramming recording horns into their beery faces. Thereby they preserved for posterity authentic bucolic gibberish, much of which was later discovered to be Sanskrit.

Foremost among these folksong shock troops was young R.V.W. Holst the well-known 'varsity rugger-cricket-and-rowing blue who actually did a bit of composing too. At Cambridge he was stung waspishly by Cecil Sharp into collecting folksongs. He made a start on Wenlock Edge but took the wrong equipment — a piano, a singer and a string quartet.

Having found the right tools he worked his way eastwards, pioneering fearlessly through the Home Counties, till he reached remote Hammersmith. Here he settled down into respectability, destroying all his 'Oi'ad'er'-type cylinders at St. Paul's Girls' School where he got a job as Musical Director.

He failed the physical for Captain Scott's Antarctic Expedition but did write their theme tune (imaginatively scored for wind machine) instead. Whilst working on his London Symphony he would often meet Handel dancing in the Strand with blonde, beautiful, mother-fixated Percy 'I'm a clean Australian boy' Grainger. Together they would tiptoe through the buttercups, butterworths and banks of green willow to visit the country garden (in the lovely English village of Grez-sur-Loing) of Frederick Delius, the orange juice magnate from Bradford.

In this idyllic setting they would make Shepherd's Hey while the sun shone, listen to the First Cuckoo in Spring, and write letters to The Times. But as R.V.W. always insisted that the first cuckoo was in fact an ascending lark, their letters were never published.

In his retirement R.V.W. became a noted authority on horticulture and his Fantasia 'Greenfingers' is sprayed regularly at the Chelsea Flower Show.

FERENC LISZT
(1811 - 1886)

Liszt's father was an Hungarian goulash or steward on the estate of Prince Esterantzen. The Prince was so touched by young Franz's piano-playing that he sent him packing to Vienna. Here the little golden haired angel studied transcendentally with Czerny, and he even played to the totally deaf Beethoven who declared him a genius. His father took him to Paris, but the great Cherubini refused the cherub's admission to the Conservatoire because he was having enough trouble already with Berlioz *(vide supra)*.

In a few years 'Le petit Litz' had become the rage of the Paris salons for his performances on the boudoir grands and their owners. A lonely foreigner in a cosmopolitan city, Liszt earned himself the nickname of 'The Thieving Magyar' for his playful habit of stealing other people's wives. He scored a great *succès de scandale* by running off with the Comtesse Marie d'Agoult, who was to bear him three children including the formidable Cosima Wagner *(née* Liszt, *mariée* von Bulow).

For a time Ferenc and Marie were radiantly happy, he accompanying her as she sang her immortal ditty, "I've got a little Liszt". But the liebestraum did not last for ever, and they separated. When Liszt rode back into Paris on his faithful horse Mazeppa, he found that a fast (crowd) drawing stranger called Thalberg had eclipsed his reputation at its high noon. There was the inevitable show-down at the Rio Bravura, both men being equipped with fast action Erards. Liszt was the better draw and won hands down.

He then became musical trouble-shooter to the Weimar Republic (sometime a Duchy), where the malicious said his reputation was even more inflated than the currency. Here eventually he got the bird on account of his latest bird, the highly eccentric Princess Carolyne Insayn Wittgenstein. Another married woman, her high camp behaviour, such as smoking cheroots, was immortalised by her lover in his famous 'La Campanatella'.

Her behaviour became increasingly bizarre, as she knitted blue stockings whilst simultaneously writing a critique of Catholicism in twenty-four massive volumes. She personally approached the Pope asking him to regularise her union with Liszt. At first he was sympathetic, but when she unwisely treated him to choice extracts from her magnum opus he gave a pious double negative (Pio Nono).

The composer showed his gratitude to Mother Church by building the celebrated Abbey Liszt, which curiously enough has vanished without trace although it has been argued that it was the original of Debussy's 'Cathédrale Engloutie'. He ended his days in an odour of sanctity and stale cigar smoke.

JEAN BAPTISTE LULLY (1632 - 1687)

Lully, the so-called Godfather of French Music, was confusingly an Italian. He was born the son of an impoverished Italian organ-grinder, often mistranslated as 'corn-grinder' and giving rise to the confusion that Signor Lully snr. was a miller. Thus it was that young Lully soon had to earn his own pasta. He studied the fiddle and three card trick in Florence, and was taken into the service of Madamoiselle d'Orléans, the notorious Mississippi Queen. His career as a small time viola da gambler was short lived, for he soon joined the outfit of 'Big Louie' (Le Grand Monarque) whose five star casino at Versailles needed a dance band leader.

Here Lully wrote many ballets, in which he and his patron, often called 'Louis the Sun Flower', partnered each other (boys will be girls). His great friend at Versailles was called Molly, and for him Lully wrote a large number of airs. These 'Molly Airs', such as 'Le Bourgeois Gentilhomme', were among his greatest successes.

In 1672, 'Big Louie' gave him a monopoly to operate the French opera racket. Lully ruthlessly cut out any rivals who tried to muscle in on what he called his 'French Connection'. His operas alone were performed at Versailles, for they had become so popular with 'Big Louie' that they were known as 'Lullypops'. Basically, the proposition in all his operas was to say to the King, "Make me the Orpheus of France and I'll praise you to Parnassus." It was an offer that 'Big Louie' couldn't refuse.

As a conductor, Lully used to give his performers and players the big stick, beating time with a gold-tipped cane. In 1687, whilst conducting a Te Deum giving thanks for 'Big Louie's' recovery from a dose of Cupid's measles, Lully in his enthusiasm skewered his foot to the podium with his cane. In this last extremity, he was apothecaried (often mistranslated as 'apotheosed') by Rameau in highly suspicious circumstances considering the prevalence of poisoning at Versailles.

GUSTAV BRUCKNER
(1824 - 1896)

Bruckner, the little Keystone comic with the treble cleft palate, was born at the back end of Austria at the back end of 1824. His father was a professional pedant who was soon pleased to note what a little swot his son was fast becoming. (Little Bruckner indeed was constantly revising, a habit he never broke).

He early discovered Wagner and literally fell at his feet. Thereafter, the Master used him as a doormat for several seasons at the Villa Wahnfried. Because of his small stature and gargoyle-like features he was highly successful both as organist and as part of the décor at the monastery of St. Florian-the-Less near Linz.

In his forties he went to Vienna and devoted himself to the composition of symphonies and more revising. In the Austrian capital he was known as 'the Teddy Bear's Picnic' for the relish with which the famous critic Edward Hanslick chewed him up.

He developed a talent for falling out of trains and being in the wrong place at the right time. Wagner called him ' Bruckner the Bungler ', sometimes mistranslated as 'Bruckner the Bugler'. Because of his gift for clowning the Emperor Franz Joseph, himself a bumbling old buffer, invited him to spend the last part of his life as court jester at the Belvedere Palace.

Bruckner was so busy revising his last symphony, dedicated (with an eye on the future) to God, that he forgot he hadn't finished it. . . . .

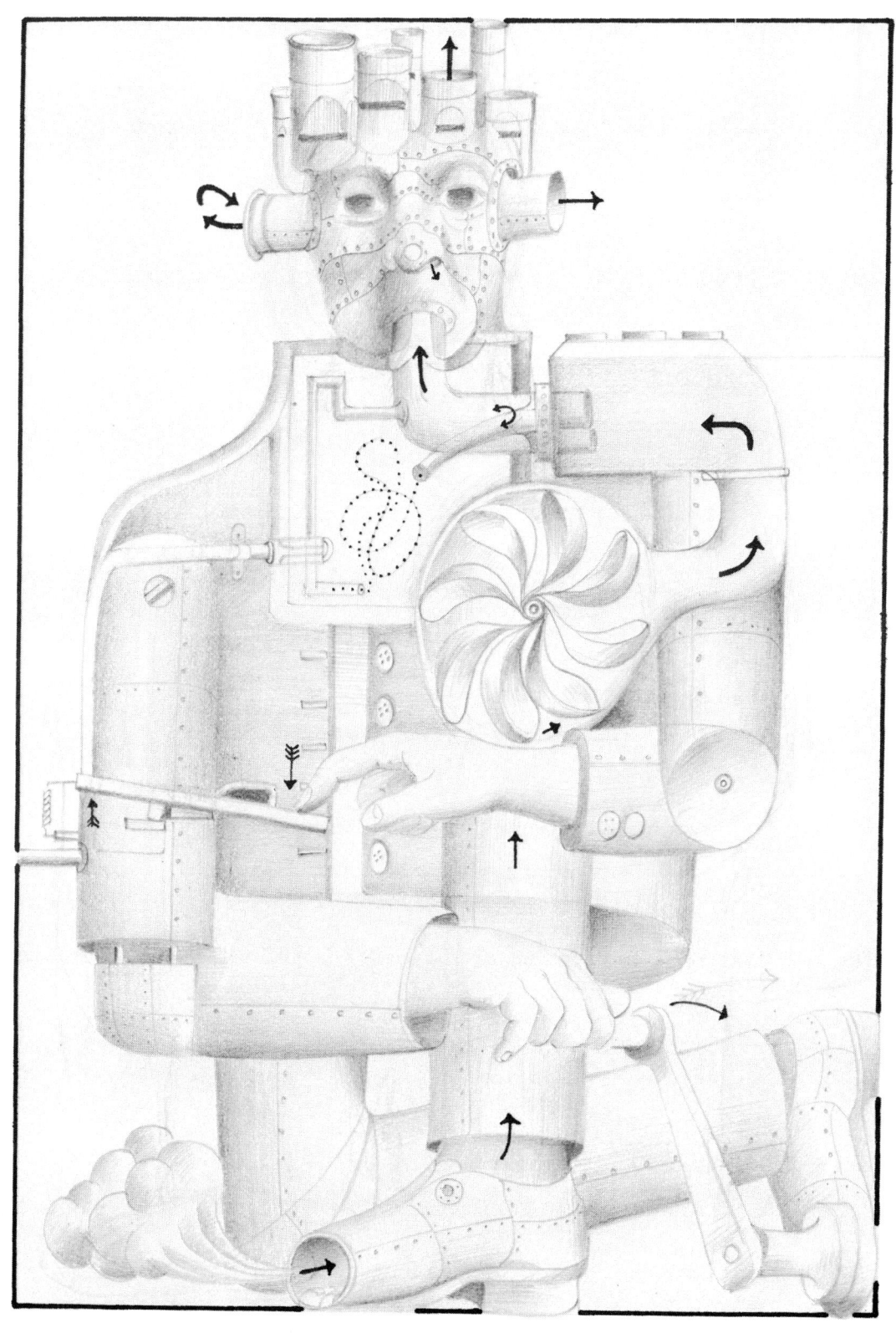

**ANTON MAHLER
(1860 - 1911)**

Meanwhile the much younger Mahler had been born at the back end of Bohemia, but soon wished that he hadn't.

Anton Mahler was known as the 'A.E. Housman of music' for his irrepressible pessimism, and his compositions are permeated with funeral marches, dead children and undertakers.

His 2nd symphony — 'The Resurrection' has been dismissed as an aberration or necrophilia — or possibly both. He was a gifted conductor with a sure grasp of orchestras and orchestration, and the vast resources that his works call for — as well as their profound gloom — have made him one of the most popular of composers with the Musicians' and Morticians' Unions. Indeed 'The Song of the Earth' was written to a commission from the latter. Like Bruckner his last symphony (No. 10) is unfinished.

Bruckner and Mahler, the Tweedledum and Tweedledee of the late Romantic symphony, agreed to have a battle to see who could write the longest, grandest composition. Mahler cheated by employing an unfairly large number of musicians, but Bruckner replied by composing symphonies called 'O' and '½' to confuse his rival — and everyone else.

Honours are even between them, although Mahler has outsmarted Bruckner by posthumously getting a musicologist to cooke up a completion of **his** unfinished symphony, known as the 'Rigor Mortis'.

Sir FELIX MENDELSSOHN, BART.
(1809 - 1847)

Sir Felix Mendelssohn, Bart., otherwise known as Prince Albert, was born with a silver tuning fork in his mouth. Most unfairly, his father was not a struggling and/or drunken musician but a highly successful Hamburg banker. Despite the signal disadvantage of a happy and extremely wealthy family background, young Felix soon showed prodigious musical promise already. The poet Goethe gave the lad an illegible Beethoven manuscript "to see Werther he could play it". (He gave a meisterly performance). Sir Julius 'Killarney' Benedict, who knew him as a child called him, rather unfortunately, 'the Lily of Hamburg', but it is not recorded what Felix called Sir Julius.

The boy gave weekly concerts at his parents' home, where his sisters were his greatest fans, especially the eldest. At the age of seventeen he dreamed of fairies, but his parents bought him the famous Leipzig Bauhaus Orchestra to take his mind off it. At the Bauhaus he pioneered new artistic developments, as well as reviving the music of B.A.C.H. (q.v.). An inveterate tourist, he visited the British Isles ten times, the Philharmonic Society giving him highly advantageous exchange rates. Felix wrote a lot of very successful travelogue music — the 'Italian' symphony (sometimes confusingly known as 'the Pasta Roll'), the 'Scotch' symphony (a commission from the Distillers' Company), and the 'Calm Sea and Prosperous Voyage' overture (written as an antidote to sea sickness whilst suffering from packet lag in the Hebrides).

Urbane and courtly, he was a popular guest at Royal Windsor, where he diplomatically attributed all his successful compositions to Prince Albert. Queen Victoria was charmed and rewarded Felix with a bartholdy.

The grandson of Moses, Felix composed his great oratorio 'Elijah' on the advice of his father to keep the performing rights in the family. It is not often realised that Mendelssohn's very popular 'Songs without Words' (Lieder ohne Wörter) began life as a Goethe-inspired song cycle called 'Lieder von Werther', but Felix mislaid the words on a day trip to Fingal's Cave. In 1847 his elder sister died and he lost his greatest Fan. Thereafter his ratings fell off alarmingly, and he succumbed to melancholia.

WOLFGANG AMADEUS MOZART
(1756 - 1791)

Mozart, alias Kochel, was born in Salzburg, fortunately for the Festival. He was the son of the celebrated violinist and composer, Attrib Leopold Mozart. Young Wolfgang's early life was a continual struggle not to be upstaged by his pretty and talented sister Maria Anna, who shared top-billing with him in their father's very popular Teeny Touring Road Show. They played to thunderous applause from the crowned heads of Europe and the half-crowned ones of London (2/6 a time at the Swan and Hoop, Cornhill).

Of astounding virtuosity and precociousness, little Wolfgang wrote his first symphony at the age of eight, and thereby earned himself the nickname of 'Kindersymphoniker'. Attempts by debunking musicologists to attribute his early works to his father or Michael Haydn can be discounted. Whilst touring in Italy, he was given a real buck by the Pope in the form of the Golden Spur, and he was also inspired by counterpoint and vermouth, which he studied with Padre Martini.

Back in Salzburg, he entered the employment of the music-loving Archbishop, who promptly died. The new Archbishop, called Hieronymus and known as 'Bosch' for the mess-up he made of his relations with Mozart, sacked the composer for what Mozart called 'Les Petits Riens'. A great opera composer, he anticipated the needs of the modern international opera circuit by writing 'Il Seraglio' in German and 'Don Juan' in Italian. Moreover, he showed his genius by writing the sequel to Rossini's 'Barber of Seville' thirty years before the original composition.

Meanwhile, Mozart had become konzertstruck with the charms of Constanze von Weber, known affectionately as Cosi fan Tutte, whom he confusingly wedded four years before the Marriage ('Le Nozze'). Mozart suffered terribly at the hands of tradesmen creditors, for he was always short on the housekeeping despite attempts at cheeseparing economies (e.g. the four Horn Concertos). He wrote 'Die Zauberflöte' for the ladies' night of his local Masonic branch, but the Queen of the Night was not amused.

He was tied by the apron strings to produce some Funeral Music, and this, combined with the award of an R.A. (Requiem Anonymous), accelerated his decline. He died in highly confusing circumstances, being poisoned by a Russian basso called Chaliapin disguised as the composer Salieri and using tartar emetic provided by Doctor Rimsky-Korsakov. After his death, his widow reverted to her maiden name, and wrote the opera 'Der Freischütz'.

45

GIACOMO PUCCINI
(1858 - 1924)
(Every packet carries a Government Health Warning)

Giacomo Puccini the champion chain-smoker and subject of Verdi's forgotten oratorio 'Elisha' was born Luccaly in Italy, for otherwise he would have had a very silly name. His mother taught him singing by savagely kicking his shins at wrong notes and he was soon known as "the chorister with perfect crutch."

He studied music in Milan where he shared student lodgings with Pietro Mascagni. It was at this time that he took up heavy smoking to disguise the verismo smells of garlic, dubious drains, and hairy armpits. His first opera 'Le Villi' (Low Cheer Rating) caused a mild flap in the claque who thought they had come to watch the economy version of 'Giselle'. His second opera 'Edgar' (Lower Cheer Rating) was just a flop pure and simple, but at the third try he was lucky.

'Manon Lescaut' (Middle Cheer Rating) was a success, though largely because the claque thought that Massenet had written it. This was followed by 'La Bohème' (High Cheer Rating) which includes the famous fish finger song. 'Tosca' (High Cheer Rating) or 'A Policeman's Lot is not an 'Appy One' was followed by 'Madama Butterfly' (High Cheer Rating) the straight version of 'The Mikado'.

Puccini visited the U.S.A. and went to Marlboro County where the flavour is. Here he was inspired to write 'La Fanciulla del West' (Middle to Low Cheer Rating) or 'Annie Get Your Gun' about the legendary female gunslinger who shot a well-smoked Virginia tipped out of his mouth at 100 yards in a futile attempt to save him from lung cancer.

His fires of inspiration were temporarily extinguished, so he returned to Italy looking for a light only to discover that Mascagni and Leoncavallo had stolen a match on him. 'Cavalleria Rusticana' (the musical version of 'The Archers') and 'Pagliacci' ('Pal Joey') were all the rage.

But Puccini lit up again with 'Il Trittico' (Middle Cheer Rating) and puffed on with 'Turandot' (Middle to High Cheer Rating). Unhappily he over-exhaled before completing it. At the première of the latter, in the completion by Alfredo from 'La Bohème', the young conductor Tosca (no relation) Nini ended Act II with the famous words, "Here Giacomo Puccini laid down his cigarette-holder for the last time — dust to dust, ash to ash."

HENRY PURCELL
(1658 - 1695)

Henry Purcell the famous musician was born, confusingly, the son of Henry Purcell the famous musician. Like many other great English composers, young Purcell received his musical education at the Café Royal, where his musical bent was quickly spotted by the roving eye of King Charles II, who appointed him 'Keeper, Mayker, Repayrer and Tuner of Instruments to the King's Most Excellent Majestie'. For the Merrie Monarch he wrote the very popular 'Nell Gwynne Dances' (unpatriotic attempts to attribute these to a German composer should be resisted).

Nicknamed 'Flute the Bellows-mender' for his work on the royal organs, he continued his studies under Dr. John Blow. One of his most successful compositions from this organic period, the 'Trumpet Voluntary' was pirated by Jeremiah Clarke, which prompted from Purcell the celebrated remark, "Never volunteer anything". Although he thus lost the royalties on the Voluntary he stuck faithfully to royalties throughout his career, serving in turn Charles II, James II and William'n'Mary. He made a lasting impression on them all. Indeed, Queen'n'Mary, who said she ode everything to Purcell, was even en-graved by him.

Although not one of the great Restoration voyeurs like Pepys, Purcell was very interested in girls' schools. "Come away, fellow sailors" he merrily quipped as the harassed Mr. and Mrs. Josias Priest finally showed him the door of the Chelsea Girls' School after the shattering premiere of 'Dido and Aeneas'. (His place as Director of Music, incidentally, was taken by R.V.W. Holst.)

In the last years of his life Purcell wrote extensively for West End theatre managements — 'The Fairy Queen' for an all male glee club, and the original version of 'Camelot', known as 'King Arthur', for Drury Lane.

In the final reckoning Purcell's life was a washout, for he died of a chill caught in a sudden nocturnal downpour after Mrs. Purcell had locked him out of the house for raking the neighbours. Although he was an almost exact contemporary of the great French composer Lully, the two men were unimpressed and uninfluenced by each other. As Lully remarked, overlooking a Purcell score, "Chaconne à son gout".

GIOACCHINO ROSSINI
(1792 - 1868)

Rossini, the celebrated bon viveur, bon homme, bon mot-elier and bon-bon, or lollipop man, leaped to fame by being born on 29th February 1792 and dying 76 years later at the confusing age of 19. His father, the town trumpeter of Pesaro, was imprisoned for his Bonapartist sympathies, shown by persistently playing the 'Eroica' instead of Leonore No. 3. His mother, who has been variously called a gypsy and an opera singer (possibly the original Azucena), took young Gioacchino to Bologna, where he studied music and sauce-making (Bolognese). Although highly adept at the former, he preferred the latter.

Food, indeed, was to become the tonic and dominant of his life. In his youth, he swept like a tournedos through the Italian opera scene, writing fifteen operas in four years, including the celebrated 'Lista di Laundri' (✗ ✗). Rossini worked himself to a crescendo, and yet he was so lazy that he allowed Mozart to write the sequel to his highly successful 'Il Barbiere di Siviglia' (✗ ✗ ✗ ✗ ✗) and even transferred the overture from 'Elizabetta' (✗) to the 'Barber'. Indeed this habit of stealing glittering titbits from his old compositions earned him the nickname of 'The Thieving Magpie'.

In the early 1820s he was invited to Paris by 'Le Comte Ory' (✗ ✗ ✗) and was very well received. In Paris he planned to write five operas, and he managed to complete the patriotic and incendiary 'Guillaume Tell' (✗ ✗ ✗ ✗ ✗) just in time for the 1830 Revolution, only to discover that Auber's 'Masaniello' had had an even more inflammatory effect in Brussels.

Disenchanted, he abandoned music for the chef d'oeuvre of his life — cooking. Already a holder of the cordon rouge of Legion d'honneur, he sought the accolade of the cordon bleu and won it with the immortal 'Tournedos Rossini' (✗ ✗ ✗ ✗) a delicious preparation of fillet steak, medium rare or 'Semiraride' (✗ ✗), in a Tancredible sauce. The aged composer of 'La Cenerentola' (✗ ✗ ✗) became the fairy pumpkin to several struggling young composers, like Saint-Saëns and Wagner, both of whom were inspired by his Cygne à l'Orange.

Famous as a humourist, he hailed Offenbach as the 'Mozart of Hades' after trying the latter's 'Pear Hélène', and he whimsically called a botched omelette, 'Une Petite Messe'. In extreme old age he indulged in his so-called "pèches de mon age" (Sins of Senility), the famous of whom was the very young Australian soprano and toast of Paris, Nellie Melba.

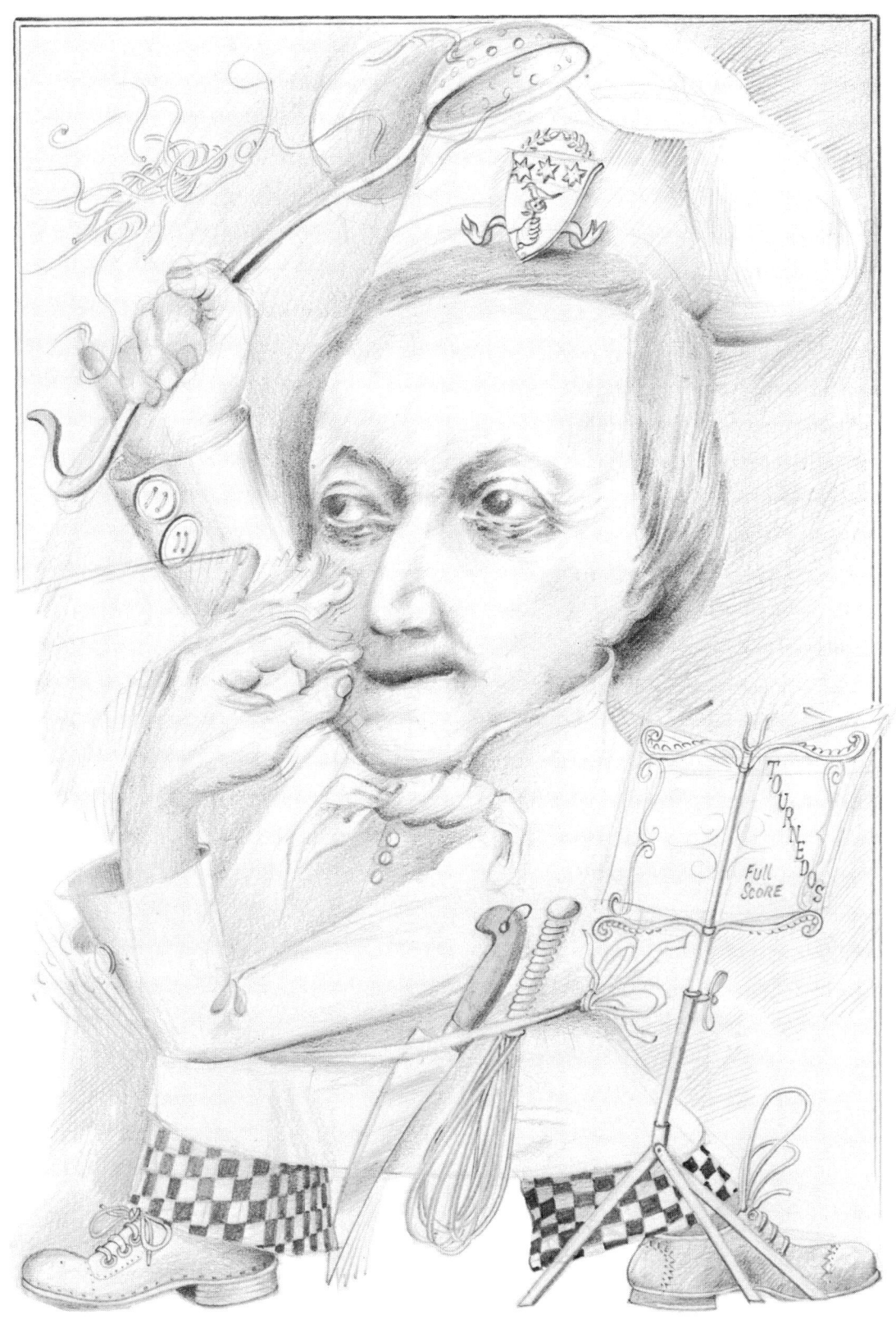

'THE FIVE' (5) or 'LES SIX' (6)
(1833 - 197-)

Much confusion exists over these supposedly two separate groups of composers until it is realised that they are, in fact, one and the same (or rather, five and six and the same). The group was first formed in Tsarist Russia to promote vodka in music, and consisted of Balakirev (their leader, and known affectionately as 'Millie'), Borodin (known as 'Baubles, Bangles and Beads'), the forthright and candid César Cui (sometimes called 'César Frank'), the retiring and modest Mussorgsky, and Rimsky-Korsakov (the bespectacled doctor of the Battleship Potemkin).

They met regularly to write each other's moujik (e.g. 'The Flight of the Flea'), compare notes on vodka ("Have another Glazunov!"), and be extremely rude to Anton Rubinstein. They were anxious to promote an ethnic Russian folk sound and were consequently known as "the Cecil Sharps of the flat Steppes".

The group fled to Paris at the time of the Bolshevik Revolution, changed their names to avoid being traced by the K.G.B., and rejuvenated themselves with large doses of Erik Satie, 'le jazz' and 'le cocktail'. Now reformed as 'Les Six' (one extra 'pour la route'), they called themselves Milhaud, Honegger, Durey, Tailleferre, Poulenc and Auric, and they continued to write one another's musique.

This had led certain critics into the foolish error of imagining that Honegger's (Borodin's) 'Pacific 231' refers to an American transcontinental express, whereas in fact the symphonic poem treats of a trans-Siberian run from St. Petersburg to the Pacific port of Vladivostok through the Steppes of Central Asia.

Although, like many White Russian exiles, they frequently quarrelled — this was known as 'biche-ing' — they opened a popular restaurant. It was called 'Le Cocteau d'Or' after Rimsky's successful opera. Here the Parisian smart set would enjoy the speciality of the house, 'le boeuf Stroganoff sur le toit'. Continued confusion as to the identify of the group has given rise to the idiom "everything is at fives and sixes". The fact that this is often rendered "sixes and sevens" only exacerbates the confusion.

ARNOLD SCHOENBERG and Sons (1874 - 1951)

Arnold Schoenberg, the tireless champion of equal rights for tones, was moved early in life by the discriminatory division of the notes on the keyboard into black and white. Although his early compositions like 'Ein Kleine Verklärte Nachtmusik' were written in tonal apartheid style, he soon found the key to tonal equality in keylessness. He moved towards this in the looney tunes of 'Pierrot Lunaire'.

So-called Twelve Tone Composing gives equal importance to all notes of the chromosome scale, and composition is based on the tone row (or cod's row depending on your prejudice), the sequence of which is rigidly adhered to. Why this should be is known as the 'Y Factor'. The transformation of the keel row can be inverted or retrograded, but as this involves standing on your head and twisting your neck, Schoenberg's music — although greatly respected — has not proved very popular.

He also developed 'Sprechgesang' or Screechsong. The rise of the Nazis forced him to flee to America, where his Biblical epic 'Moses and Aaron' was rejected by Sam Goldwyn who took the Golden Calf worship as a personal criticism. Schoenberg was blacklisted and died soon after. His twelve tone work was elaborated by his 'boys', Alban Berg and Anton Webern.

Berg is best remembered for his two operas, 'Wozzeck' and 'Lulu'. The former is the well-known soldier's tale and was in fact written by Stravinsky, and the latter has the memorable title role of the Vienna roll who eventually gets unrolled by Jack the Ripper.

Webern is remembered for the microscopic 'Five Pieces for Orchestra'. Sneeze and you miss them. Unlike many Austro-German composers, Webern certainly did not benefit from the post-war American Marshall Aid Scheme: "Bang! Bang! who's there?" "An. . . " "Ann who?" "Anton Webern, ahhh!"

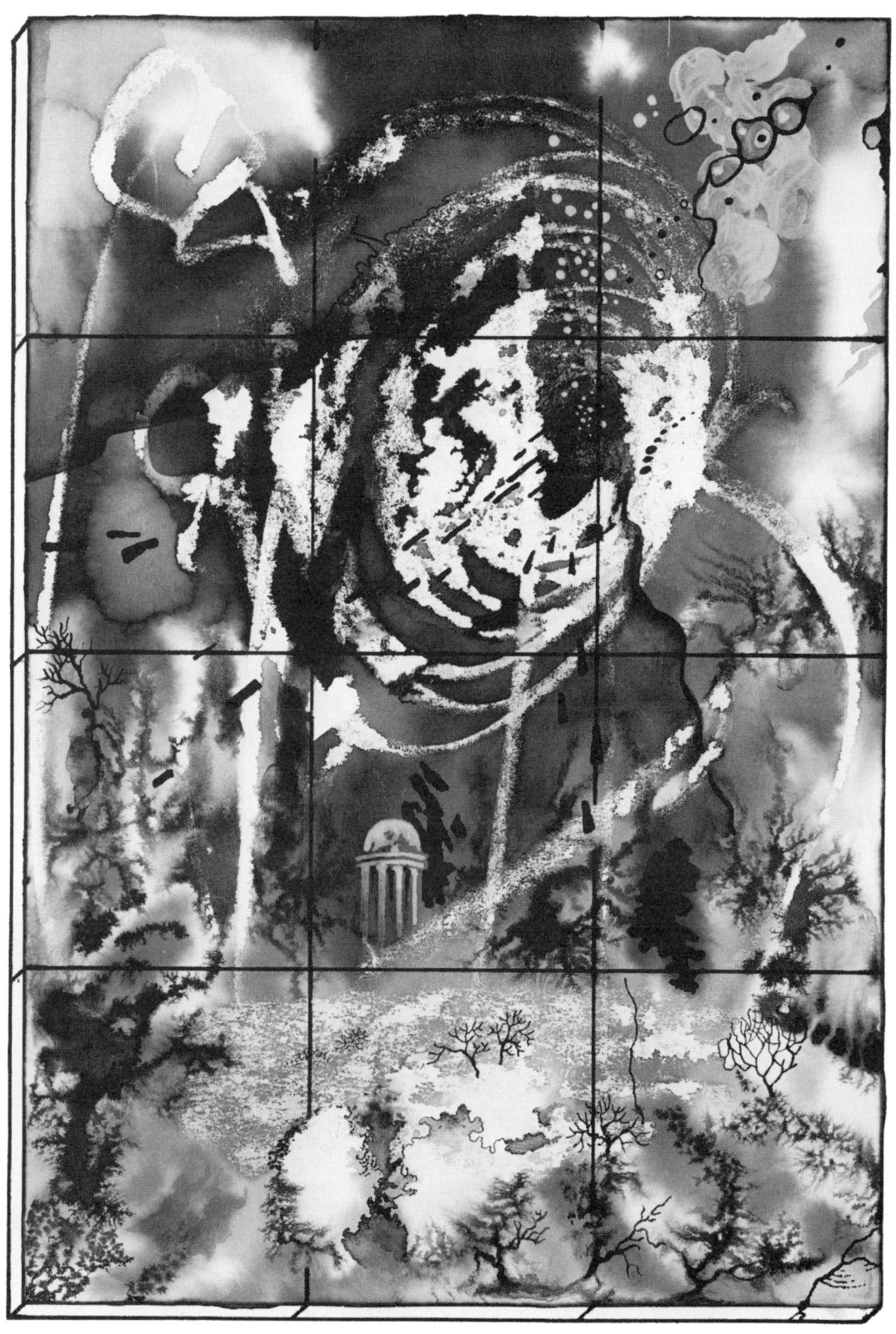

FRANZ SCHUBERT
(1797 - 1828)

Little Franz Schubert suffered from an acute inferiority complex all his life, through being put at a very early age behind a pair of National Health 'owls'. Stunted, snub-nosed and moon-faced as well as bespectacled, it is amazing that he was accepted as a choirboy, especially as he wasn't even good at games. Nevertheless he joined the Imperial Court choir and studied for a time with the composer Salieri whose poisonous reputation was well known *(Vide* Mozart *supra)*.

Schubert survived, but not for long. His life was short but highly productive. He became the leader of the lieder movement, composing over 600 songs, including 'Gretchen at the Spin-drier', 'Die Schöne Müllerin' ('Trooble oop a' t' mill'), the self-mocking 'Who is sillier?', the musical 'We'll gather Lilac Time' and 'The Song of the Vogl Boatman'. This last piece was written for his great friend Michael Vogl, the famous voglist, for whom he wrote many bicycling songs. These he and Vogl performed on a tandem, and the best known is the 'Winterreise' cycle with its lovely setting of 'Daisy, Daisy'.

Meanwhile he had become music master to Count Johann Esterantzen's lonely and consumptive daughter, whom Schubert called 'das Mädchen on her Tod'. It was a hopeless passion and when the old Countess took the 'Trout' Quintet as a personal insult, Schubert was shown the door. Although never robust or truly athletic, he earned modest fame as a sprinter for his celebrated hundred yard dashes in the opposite direction whenever he saw Beethoven.

He was a popular guest at Viennese musical evenings at which he would do one of his 'impromptu' turns, such as not turning up or wandering off into a fantasy and falling off the piano-stool. He was hopelessly vague, forgetting to finish one symphony and completely mislaying another whilst holidaying in Gastein, mumbling that he thought he had left it in the Grand Duo (Hotel). He advertised for a conductorship — the so-called Schubertiads — but was unsuccessful, and he wandered off on his tod at the early age of 31.

ROBERT SCHUMANN (1810 - 1856)

Robert Schumann (alias Florestan, alias Eusebius, alias Robert Browning) the well-known schizophrenic and Rhine-swimmer was born at Zwickau in Saxony. The son of a publisher, he devoured books from an early age and "developed strong literary tastes". He plunged into everything with romantic abandon including, as we shall see, rivers.

He early developed a distressing habit of writing newspaper articles telling perfect strangers to take off their hats, which made people fear for his sanity. He studied piano and aquatics with little Clara Barrett Wieck, the 'Shirley Temple of the keyboard' and one of the famous 'Wiecks von der Wimpolestrasse'.

Her father, the well-known swimming coach, caught them at it, and Robert was shown the door. He was unimpressed and formed the Davidsbündler to bang on the knocker of Wimpolestrasse, shout "Philistine!" through the letterbox and run away.

He understandably became increasingly worried about his fourth finger and tried a postal tendon-building course — "Are you a fourth finger weakling? Do arpeggios kick sand in your face?" — with unfortunate results. He gave up the piano and concentrated on banging knockers — with even more unfortunate results.

He continued to take off his hat to everybody including Sterndale Bennett, which made people fear for his sanity still more. At the age of 30 he married his Clara, the daughter of the well-known swimming coach, who had opposed the match on the grounds that Robert's butterfly was no match for Clara's breast-stroke.

Always literary minded, Robert wrote a series of 'Novellettes' but nobody could read them except Clara, who played them on the piano. This made people begin to have their doubts about her. In 1852 Robert plunged into the Rhine seeking inspiration for a new 'Rhenish Symphony', but this German Romantic All-Comers' Melody Freestyle record was disallowed by Coach Wieck who demanded a dope test. Robert was found to be on mercury at the time, the result of his youthful knocker-banging, and was confined in a hydropathic asylum, where he died two years later of water on the brain.

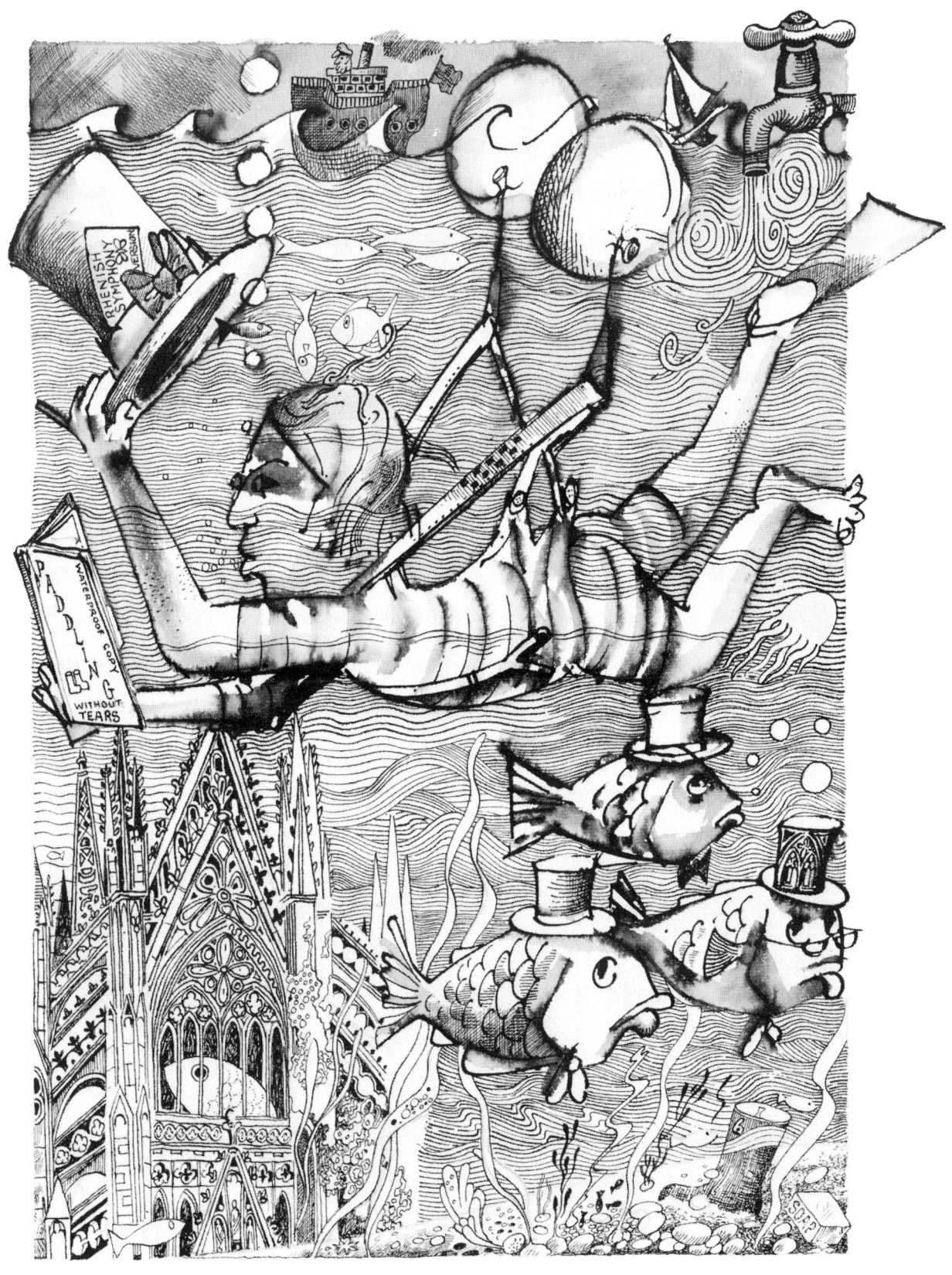

SOUSA & CO. INC.
Hail Columbus!

Just as the Spaniards got foreigners to do their composing, so it was the Italian Columbus who discovered America for them. He was greeted on arrival with the popular anthem 'Hail Columbus', but he upset his hosts by speaking Chinese and heisting all their bullion.

The first authentic American musical voice was that of Louis Moreau Gottschalk, who unfortunately only spoke French, German and Spanish. His habit of eloping with heiresses to the Caribbean earned him the nickname of 'the Cuban heel'. So confused were his amours and musical identity that it was said of him that he couldn't tell chalk from a cheeseburger.

Someone who could at least tell chalk from burnt cork and who is often hailed as the Daddy of American Music was Stephen 'Mammy' Foster, owner ob de Camptown Races, de Old Folks and various other Doo-Dahs. Indeed his unfortunate habit of exposing himself at the Camptown Races is immortalised in the song 'Zipperdy-Doo-Dah'.

Edward MacDowell, 'the American Grieg', failed because he was too tall *(vide Grieg supra)* and also like Gottschalk he spoke German.

It is often overlooked that, behind the bluff bandmaster image, Sousa was the ruthless founder of the forerunner of the C.I.A. His surname was the initial code of "Secrets Office, United States of America". His part in the assassination of President Garfield in March 1881, after which he was known as 'the March King', is ambivalent, and why else was he often called 'leader of all the president's men?' Perhaps one day the Washington Post will tell. Finally, Sousa's immigrant origins lay him so open to the charge that he was in the pay of the Tsarist Okrana that he cannot be considered 100% American.

The man who really insured an original and authentic American voice was ace insurance salesman Charles Ives. And yet even here his so-called revolutionary composing technique was in fact his Puritan New England frugality which made him compose several pieces simultaneously on the same sheet of manuscript.

After the Great War, several American ex-servicemen studied in Paris with Nadia Boulanger and were consequently known as Doughboys, although curiously enough George Gershwin was not one of these Parisian Americans. The most famous of them was Aaron Cowhand, the rawhide Rodeo rider, whose cowboy ballet 'Billy Budd' has been criticised for its unhappy setting as an opera on a Nelsonian warship.

Finally the most eloquent of contemporary American composers is the skittish John Cage, whose tantalising '4 Minutes 33 Seconds' is eagerly awaited in a full length version.

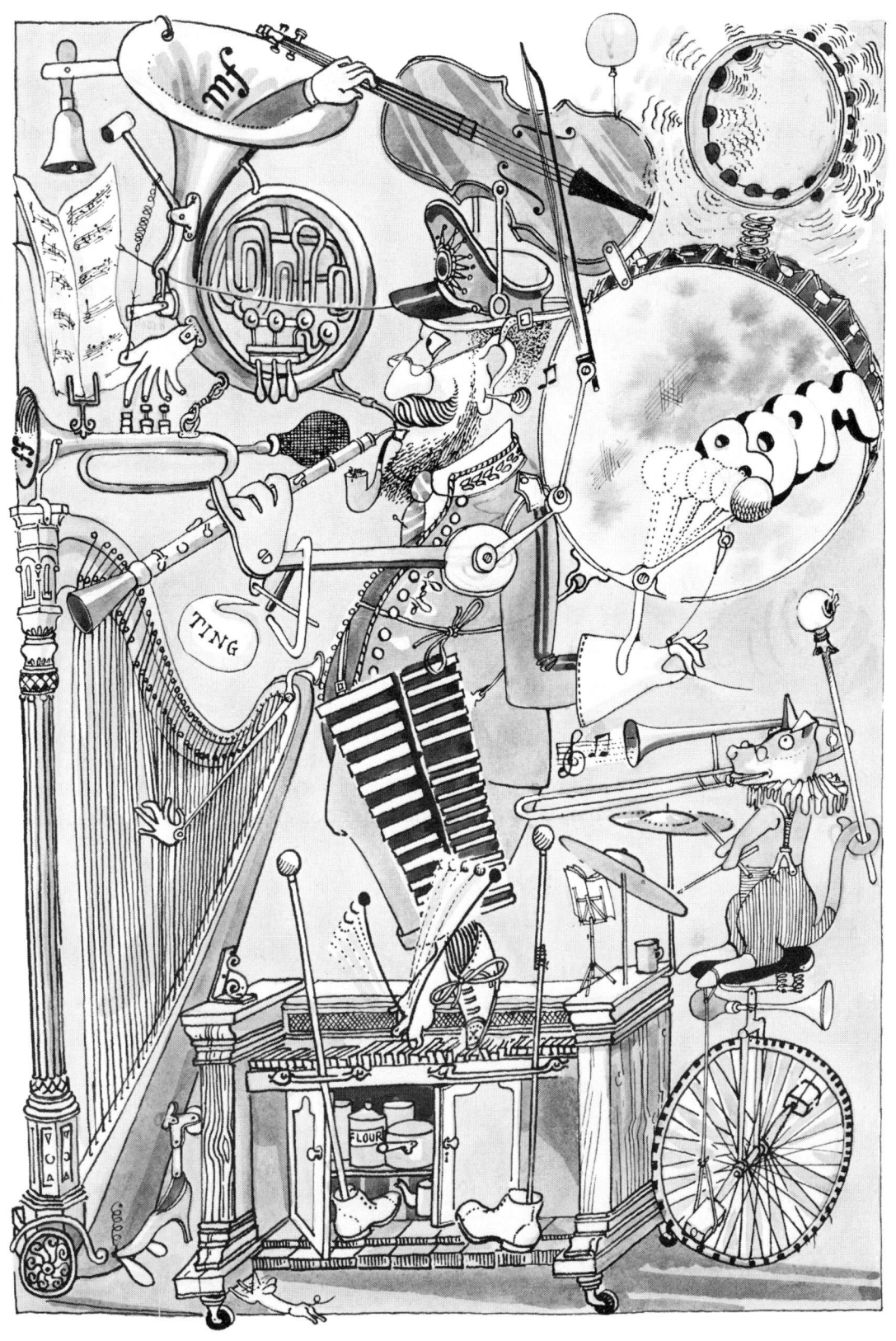

THE COMPLEAT STRAUSS
(1804 - 1949)

Around the beginning of the nineteenth century began the so-called 'Sturm and Strauss' period in German artistic life. When the storm abated, the serene and sunny Strauss family shone brightly and lightly on the Viennese musical scene.

Founder of the fortunes of this remarkable dynasty was Joseph Lanner, the original Viennese wurlitzer, who was always ready to ländler hand to his first violinist, Johann Sebastian Strauss the Elder. This composer is best remembered for writing Berlioz's Hungarian March, known as the 'Razumovsky' and sometimes attributed to Beethoven. The Elder Strauss was, like the similarly forenamed B.A.C.H. a marathon parent, producing a vast brood of younger Strausses, all lustily beating their rattles in 3/4 time whilst still in their cradles.

Most famous of the younger Strausses was Johann Sebastian Strauss the Younger, whose 'Waltz King's Rhapsody' was published by Ivor Novellos. Other best-loved rhapsodies include 'Tales from the Vienna Woods' (the original site of the Teddy Bears' Picnic) and the 'Dan Yewb Blues' written to celebrate the great Australian bushwhacker, and subsequently known as 'Waltzing Matilda' (after Dan's sheila). Although many of his works were contemptuously dismissed by the critics in the morning papers as 'a load of tritsch-tratsch', he didn't fledermaus an eyelid but invited his brother Joe to have a go at composing, too. Success came swiftly with 'Village Swallows' and together the brothers picked yet another winner with 'Pizzicato Polka'. Even baby brother Eduard jumped on to the Strauss bandwagon.

About this time, the first horn of the Munich Court Orchestra, Franz Strauss (no relation, though related to his son) became the father of Richard Strauss, the most original and successful of the post-Wagnerian Wagnerians. In his early period Richard collaborated with the poet Victor Hugo in a series of operas known as 'The Tales of Hofmannsthal', the most popular of which was 'Der Rosenkavalier' or 'The Man from Interflora'.

Latterly settled in domestic bliss at Garmisch he modestly wrote 'Ein Heldenleben' and taught himself to read Zoroastrian, saying that at last he'd found his nietzsche.

Other twentieth century Strausses have included Hollywood Oscar Strauss, Johann Sebastian Strauss the Even Younger and Claude Lévi-Strauss (no relation, not even a gene.)

IGOR STRAVINSKY
(1882 - 1971)

Stravinsky, the celebrated horse-trainer and Parisian Big Store magnate, was born at Oranienbaum near St. Petersburg, later Petrograd and now Leningrad. Understandably he became disorientated early in life and spent most of his maturity in the Occident. His father was a bass at the Imperial Opera, but little Igor was told to study law. At the University, however, he soon threw over tort to be taught composition by Rimsky-Korsakov.

He exploded onto the Russian musical scene like a fire-cracker, and rose like a 'Oiseau de Feu' from the flames of his 'Feux d'Artifice'. The man who lit Stravinsky's blue touch-paper was Sergey Diaghilev, the Rasputin of the Russian Ballet, whose magnetic charm mesmerised the greatest creative talents of Russia to join forces in his confusingly named Ballets Russes de Paris (subsequently Monte Carlo).

Shoulder to shoulder and Bakst to Bakst, this great enterprise opened in the Paris of 1909 to rapturous applause. In the first season, Stravinsky chopped up and rearranged some Chopin pieces ('Chopsticks' later known as 'Les Sylphides'), but the bouquets went to Pavlova and her performing dogs who took the bisquits with their well-conditioned responses.

The following season saw Diaghilev and Stravinsky, both keen men of the turf, at Longchamps for the races with their legendary colt, Nijinsky. This immortal creature won the hearts of Paris, despite an alarming tendency to jump through windows on hearing orchestrations by Berlioz. Indeed, this legendary and triumphant arched leap won them the so-called 'Prix de l'Arc de Triomphe'.

By now a rich man, Stravinsky went into Big Store management, taking over the famous 'Au Printemps' in 1913 and announcing the greatest sale reductions ever. There ensued the notorious 'Sack au Printemps' caused by over-enthusiastic bargain hunters running amok and wrecking the place.

Unable to return to Russia because of the Revolution, Stravinsky took French nationality, went through a neo-classical revival (which several critics diatonically panned), and then took his craft to the U.S.A., where one was already waiting for him. Here he worked on the 'Apollon' Space Programme (falsely attributed to Richard Strauss), lamented with Jeremiah on twelve-tone composing, and, remembering his Nijinsky days, endowed the American turf classic known as the 'Dumbarton Oaks'.

GILBERT 'N' SULLIVAN
(1836 - 1911)
or The Lad that loved a Lozenge

The chicken or the egg, the horse or the cart, Cox or Box, Gilbert or Sullivan? Let it be said at the outset so that there will be no further confusion that Gilbert wrote the words (when it wasn't F.C. Burnand, Julian Sturgis or Basil Hood) and Sullivan wrote the music. The composer Sir Arthur Seymour Gilbert started out as a choirboy at the Café Royal where he narrowly escaped being assaulted by Oscar Wilde (with patience he was later to get his revenge).

Arthur continued his studies at Leipzig where he ran into and tripped over Grieg (q.v.), the well-known midget, and fell all over him. Returning to England he became a serious composer, writing the 'Oirish' Symphony, a boggling achievement. Meanwhile the playwright and wit William Schwenk Sullivan, after being cradle-snatched by the Pirates of Pesaro, had become a lawyer, though he resisted the blandishments of the attorney's elderly ugly daughter. He was called to the bar of the Savoy where he met Arthur Gilbert and Richard Doiley Carte, a young entrepreneur who had just made a fortune out of paper tea table decorations, and was anxious to promote English opera as far as it would go. In his own words, "A laugh, a tune, and some handsome receipts. Sign here and here, lads!"

The result was the Savoy Operas, all the way from the Breach-of-Promise Court to the Court of the Grand Duke by way of Titipu. Carte was in clover or at least cabbages, but Sullivan and Gilbert were locked in an acrimonious personality clash. It started when Gilbert attempt to recast his 'Oirish' Symphony as a Gaelic ballad opera 'Mickey Doh, or The Fiddler of Dooney,' but Sullivan knackered it and lacquered it as 'The Mikado', the comic version of 'Madama Butterfly'.

Things grew worse as Gilbert refused to swallow any more of Sullivan's comic lozenges and proceed to write a serious grand opera. The result was 'Ivanhoe', the world's longest consecutively running opera, though virtually unrevived after the first run as Sullivan noted with grimsdyke satisfaction. Disappointed at the tarnishing of the golden legend of his serious reputation, Gilbert died whilst working on 'The Emerald Isle', the longed for reshaping of the 'Oirish' Symphony, which was appropriately finished by German. Sullivan was an early victim of the excitement of mixed bathing for he tried a stroke too many in his pool with two young ladies.

PYOTR ILYICH TCHAIKOVSKY (1840 - 1893)

Tchaikovsky was born in Votkinsk in the Urals, where his father was the very model of a mining Major-General. Young Pyotr studied rudiments with a musical box, but when the cranes flew the family moved to the capital, leaving three of his sisters behind. Pyotr became a clerk in the Justice Ministry, where he was told to chekov piles of police reports, but he was so upset by Crime and Punishment that he resigned and studied counterpoint and cosmetics with Helena Rubinstein.

A promising young composer, he quarrelled with 'The Five' *(vide supra)*, the celebrated group of nationalist Russian composers, who regarded him as a decadent Westerner and despised him for his powerful aversion to vodka, limiting himself as he did to One gin. He was pushkin to his disastrous marriage by simultaneously writing and receiving a letter aria (the celebrated 'Letter Duet' wrongly attributed to Mozart). He found it difficult to relate to his wife and they separated after nine weeks of married mayhem.

At this time, Tchaikovsky was working on his first great ballet, 'Swan Lake', and seeking inspiration he took a leaf out of Rothbart Schumann's swimming manual and plunged into the Neva (this is often erroneously referred to as a suicide attempt). The ballet was badly received, on the grounds that the music was too symphonic, which was surprising considering that the choreography was by the Tsar himself (the 'Little Father' or Petit pa').

As a symphonist, Tchaikovsky has been cruelly called 'The little Russian of pathetic Polish Winter Daydreams'. Down on his luck, Dame Fortune (Pique Dame) smiled on him in the person of Nadezhda von Meck, the great patroness of the arts, who gave many struggling artists 'bread' and was consequently known as 'Nadezhda Boulanger'. She gave him an allowance of 6000 roubles a year until she discovered Debussy *(vide supra)*. In 1893, Cambridge University awarded honorary doctorates to five famous composers. The 'Russian Five' naturally turned up and were incensed to see the awards to go to Saint-Saëns, Bruch, Boito, Grieg and Tchaikovsky.

Later the same year, Tchaikovsky, suffering from a little gastric upset, took the notorious water cure that killed him. It has been maliciously circulated that Tchaikovsky was homosexual. This is easily disproved by the fact that, when in Paris, he met a girl called Celeste (known affectionately as 'Sugar Plum') whom he had taken secretly back to Russia for his own exclusive use, being particularly anxious that Rimsky-Korsakov and Glazunov shouldn't get their hands on her.

GUISEPPE VERDI
(1813 - 1901)

The origins of Joe Green, as he was laughingly known (though he never found it very funny himself), present a classic case of Gilbertian baby-farming. He was born Vittorio Emanuele Re d'Italia, but, in one of the many confused upheavals that punctuated the 'Rigoletto' or nineteenth century Rebirth of Italy, he was cradle-switched with a peasant lad of repellent aspect. This was done, incidentally, by a red-shirted revolutionary disguised as a biscuit. His foster parents were peasant shopkeepers, and little Giuseppe quickly adopted their attitudes. "I ham from Parma," he would proudly say in later years.

His father, as the name suggests, was a greengrocer, and the enterprising lad taught himself musical rudiments on the spinanch. (Unfortunately the technique has subsequently been lost). He failed the entrance examination to the Milan Conservatoire and decided accordingly to become a composer. After some early struggles with Signora Destino, his demanding landlady, he eventually scaled La Scala with the hit musical 'No No Nabucco'. This is justly famous for its heart-busting SATB arrangement of Psalm 137, although curiously this has been totally ignored by English cathedral choirs.

Verdi now devoted himself almost entirely to the theatre, composing over thirty operas which were to keep impresarios, town bands and organ-grinders in business for years to come. Generally speaking he went from strength to strength, but he did run into trouble from the censor's office with his controversial gay opera, 'Un Ballo in Mascara' ('A Drag Ball'). The slight to the Swedish royal family was considered too strong, but it was perfectly acceptable when he changed it to the English aristocracy. Accordingly his name was mud in England, until 'Il Vespiri' with its lovely setting of 'Christopher Robin is saying his prayers' won the hearts of middle-class English mothers.

Delightfully, Joe married Jo. She was the strapping soprano, Giuseppina Strepponi, and should not be confused with the heroine of 'Little Women'. About 1870 Verdi, following the success of 'Attila' with its Venetian setting, designed the Suez Canal as part of the Italian Government's Aid-a-Plan for the Khedive of Egypt. Unfortunately French propaganda has successfully claimed credit for this on behalf of an obscure Gallic composer called de Lesseps. Moreover, the French circulated the diabolical rumour that Verdi's last two operas were written by Mephistopheles. This was done at the instigation of Gou know who. Serenely indifferent, Joe and Jo ended their days in the devoted care of Aggie, their saintly daily, known locally as Sant'Agata.

ANTONIO VIVALDI
(1675 - 1741)

Vivaldi, the well known crypto-communist and revolutionary leader of the Italian Baroque, was born in Venice, where his father was known as 'the fiddler on the roof' for his performances high in the galleries of St. Mark's. Young Antonio was a bright young spark, and he was known in Venice as 'the Artful Doger' for his seditious attitude towards the chief city magistrate. Something of a chip off the old Cremona, he studied stradivariously with his father. Later he became the pupil of the great Guevarra Legrenzi, known as 'Che', with whom he studied harmony, counter-revolution and urban terrorism.

In order to form his first activist cell, he entered the local seminary and read for the church, where his socialist sympathies earned him the disapproval of his superiors and the nickname of 'the Red Dean'. Somewhat surprisingly, he found his vocation with the foundling girls of the Ospedale della Pietà, where musically gifted orphan girls were given a thorough grounding and played regularly in the church orchestra. Vivaldi, as their musical director, disseminated his talents among the orphan orpheans, desperately keeping his standards up in over four hundred concertos. Not surprisingly he was accused of grosso behaviour and he resigned from the Ospedale a baroquen man.

He associated with Tartini for a time, but the neighbours accused them of diabolism and they fled North pursued by the Inquisition in a trilling chase. Vivaldi tried his luck in Vienna, but ill fortune continuoed to beset him and he made a ritornello to Italy for a fine, that after his Ospedale days, was definitely more of a whimper than a bagnio.

He ended his days as an itinerant frozen confectionery salesman, the original 'Antonio and his icecream cart'. As a composer he was profoundly influenced by his older contemporaries, Corelli, Torelli and Pirelli. Indeed he wrote his best loved work, 'The Four Seasons', at the instigation of the latter for inclusion in one of the celebrated Pirelli calendars. In his turn, he profoundly influenced Bach, who wrote many compositions inspired by the great Venetian and consequently known as Bacharoles.

RICHARD WAGNER
(1813 - 1883)

Richard Wagner (GENIUS) discovered it very early in life and never left off blowing his own tuba. As a young man he played with the fairies ('Die Feen') only to discover that they preferred Mendelssohn, a traumatic experience for which he never forgave the 'fairy dew'.

Always a pioneer, he reached new heights by launching the Dutch airline K.L.M. Despite the availability of a Norwegian stewardess called Senta, it crashed at the Paris Opera, allowing a receiver named Meyerbeer to move in and do some prophète taking. Wagner's one comic opera, 'Die Meistersinger von Nürnberg' was dismissed by the critic Hanslick as 'a load of cobblers'.

In 1848 Wagner flirted with liberal revolutionaries, but soon found that maniac conservative absolutists were more to his liking. He was patronized by a genial kulturomaniac called Ludwig II of Cloud Cuckoo Land, on whose castles Wagner worked as an interior decorator, embellishing the mouldings with leitmotifs and designing the highly successful wallpaper known as 'Lohengrin'. Unhappily in 1886 Ludwig fell overboard during a swan-upping trip on Lake Starnberg and was drowned.

Meanwhile (!) Wagner, ever anxious to help a struggling fellow musician, took Von Bülow's wife off his Hans so that the latter could concentrate on copying the parts of 'Götterdämmerung'. Cosima then concentrated on Wagner's. Having thus enlisztedher (his Gesamtkunstwerk) to work in the box office and cook the books (the notorious 'Siegfried Fiddle') he opened a little wooden shack at Bayreuth where he staged his ever popular summer seasons of circus in 'Der Ring' and pierrot shows like 'Parsifal Lunaire'.

He died in Venice as a result of hearing a gondolier playing Siegfried's funeral music on a mandolin.

CARL MARIA VON WEBER (1786 - 1826)

The ambiguously forenamed creator of Romantic opera was born weak and sickly, a condition that was later exacerbated by his penchant for nitric acid cocktails. He first came to fame as being the only composer to have learnt the 'Almanach de Gotha' and 'Baedeker's Guide to the Confederation of the Rhine' by heart — and understand them.

Not only was he able to travel with unerring ease and accuracy from Breslau to Karlsruhe to Stuttgart to Darmstadt to Munich to Berlin to Württemberg to Dresden to Karlsbad and back to Dresden, again, but young Weber could also distinguish (in their natural habitat) between the Duke of Schleswig-Meiningen-Saxe-Strelitz and the Margrave of Baden-Baden-Baden. He also knew the relationship between the Electress of Pillnitz and the Graf von Bierwurst-Blutenbottel (but kept quiet about it).

Weber and his impecunious father toured the princely courts as itinerant composer-musicians fleeing their creditors. For a time they took refuge with the genial transvestite Duke of Saxe-Gotha who disguised them as chamber music maids. Later, young Weber was patronised by Duke Eugen Friedrich of Württemberg who commended him to his brother Duke Ludwig of Württemberg, but the composer was not sure that this was getting him anywhere.

Success came at last in 1816 with performances of his cantata 'Kampf and Sieg', which despite its unfortunately proto-Nazi-sounding title brought him the patronage of King Friedrich August of Saxony and the directorship of the Dresden Opera. Here he wrote a cantata for the marriage of the Princess Maria Anna Carolina of Saxony to the Grand Duke Leopold of Tuscany, the 'Jubel' Overture for King Friedrich's golden jubilee, masses for the Royal birthdays and wedding anniversaries, and incidentally 'Der Freischütz'. In this the important solo part for musket was considered a very daring innovation and the opera was regarded by the reactionaries as a diabolical liberty.

After this Weber suffered from a severe attack of libretti that undermined his already delicate health. First there was 'The Three Pintas' (to a commission from the Dresden Milch Marketing Board) and then 'Euryanthe' (incidentally to a librett by 'Rosamunde' von Chezy, that formidable pioneer of Women's Libs).

Finally Weber travelled to England for 'Oberon' (a Panto for Covent Garden cobblé par M. Planché). When Weber realised that doubling as the rear-end of the horse was written into his contract, he immediately expired and was put under grass at Moorfields.

Eighteen years later Dresden realised he was dead and asked him back. He was reinterred at an emotionally trauermatic ceremony with Richard Wagner acting as an extremely eloquent mute.

HEINZ-ATTILA DOPPELKLANGER and DISSONANTE AVANTI-GUARDIA
(1928 -   )   (1924 -   )

Doppelklanger and Avanti-Guardia are justly hailed as the leaders — Führer and Duce respectively — of contemporary 'progressive' music. Their careers have followed parallel courses, but latterly in their electronic phase they have fused.

Doppelklanger studied essential rudiments (1943 - 45) at the Krupp Munitions Factory, where his explosive talent was first seen in his Opus V1 and Opus V2. Premiered in England, they were badly received. In the early Fifties, after continuing his studies at Nuremberg and Spandau, he firmly laid the foundations of his musique concrète period with his monumental 'Concerto for Pile-Driver and Pre-Adhesive Tape', which overwhelmed critics and audience alike.

Meanwhile, south of the Alps, Avanti-Guardia, who had studied at the Milan Abattoir was taking Italian 'progressive' music by the horns. Deeply influenced by post-war theatrical trends, he boldly experimented in what he called the 'Music of Cruelty' and the 'Music of the Absurd'. In the former his remarkably painstaking attention to detail was seen in his poignant 'Agonia IV for Cat and Electronic Mangle', but this brought a storm of protest from the R.S.P.C.A. and was abandoned after the first performance.

Nothing daunted, he experimented in Absurdist non-tonal music, and his seven hour long song-cycle 'Silencio for Deaf-Mute and Dummy Keyboard' was given a standing ovation by the entire audience of three fellow experimental composers at the Cracow Progressive Music Symposium in 1963.

By the early Seventies the enormous talents of these gifted composers had been brought together, and they are currently living together in Bermuda, working on joint compositions. Their celebrated laughing song 'All the Way to the Bank' was written to a commission from the International Monetary Fund and premiered by Pierre Boules.

Their very latest work, the 'Armageddon Symphony' for 500 megaton warhead and the combined male voice choirs of the Kremlin and the Pentagon still waits its première, but with the capable fingers of Doppelklanger and Avanti-Guardia on the button, the future of music can safely be

INDEX

A
Aberdeen	27
d'Agoult, Comtesse Marie	35
Aix-la-Chapelle	29
Albert, Prince	43
Alsace Sheep Dog Trials	13
Anon (circa)	7,8
l'Arc de Triomphe	65
Arden, Forest of	17
Arno, River	13
Arthur, King	49
Auber, Daniel	51
Auric, Georges	53,54
Avanti-Guardia, Dissonante	79,80

B
B.A.C.H. Johann Sebastian	9,10,43,63,73
B.A.C.H., Johann Christian	9,10
B.A.C.H., Wilhelm Friedemann	9,10
Baedeker	77
Baden-Baden-Baden, Margrave of	77
Baker Street, no. 221b	23
Balakirev, Mily	53,54
Ballets Russe	65
Bardac, Emma	25
Beethoven, Ludwig van	11,**12**,31,43,57,63
Bellini, Vincenzo	19
Benedict, Sir Julius	43
Bennett, Sir William Sterndale	59
Berg, Alban	27,55
Berlioz, Hector	13,**14**,17,63,65
Bierwurst-Blutenbottel, Graf von	77
Birtwistle, Harrison	21
Black Death, the	7
Blow, Dr. John	49
Bohemia	21,39
Boito, Arrigo	69
Borodin, Alexander	53,54
Boulanger, Nadia	61,69
Boules, Pierre	79
Bourgeois Gentilhomme, le	37
Bowles, Sally	19
Bovril, Dr. John	17,18
Brown, John	23
Bruch, Max	15,69
Bruckner, Gustav	39,**40**,51,15
Budd, Billy	61
Bull, Ole	27
Bülow, Hans von	35,75
Burnand, F.C.	67
Burnham, Howard	85
Butterworth, George	33
Butterworth, Richard	85

C
Cage, John	61
Cambridge University	15,33,69
Camelot	49
Camptown Races, de	61
Carte, Richard Doiley	67
Cézanne, Paul	25
Chaliapin, Fyodor	45
Chandos, Duke of	29
Charles II, King	49
Chelsea Flower Show	33
Cherubini, Luigi	13,19,35
Chezy, Wilhelmine von	77
Chopin, Fryderyk	19,29,65
C.I.A.	61
Clarke, Jeremiah	49
Claus, Santa	15
Columbus, Christopher	61
Corelli, Arcangelo	73
Cowhand, Aaron	61
Croche, Monsieur	25
Cruft's Dog Show	23
Cui, Cesar	53,54
Czerny, Carl	19

D
Death, The Black	7
Debussy, Claude	25,**26**,35
Delius, Frederick	33,34
Degas, Edgar	25
Detmold	15
Diaghilev, Sergey	65
Doppelklanger, Heinz-Attila	79,80
Dowland, John	17,18
Drake, Sir Francis	17,18

Dresden Opera	77
Durey, Louis	53,54
Dvořák, Antonín	21,22

E

Edison-Bell	33
Egypt, Khedive of	71
Eiffel Tower	25
Elgar, Sir Edward	23,24
Elizabeth I, Queen	17,18
Emerson Edition	85
Enigma Variations	23
Eroica	51
Eugen Friedrich of Württemberg, Duke	77
Eugenie, Empress	23
Eulenspiegel, Till	31

F

Farnaby, Giles	17,18
Fenby, Eric	29
Fleurville, Madame de	25
Foster, Stephen	61
Franz Joseph, Emperor	39
Friedrich August, King	77

G

Garden, Mary	25
Garfield, President	61
Gaudeamus Igitur	15
George I, King	29
German, Sir Edward	67
Gershwin, George	61
Ghengis Khan	9
Gilbert, Sir Arthur	67,68
Glazunov, Alexander	53,69
Goethe, Johann Wolfgang von	43
Goldwyn, Sam	55
Gotha, Almanach de	77
Gottschalk, Louis Moreau	61
Grainger, Percy	33,34
Grand Central Station	21
Gregory, Pope	7
Grieg, Edvard	27,28,61,67,69
Gwynne, Nell	49,50

H

Hagerup, Nina	27,28
Hallelujah Chorus	29
Hammerschmidt, Andreas	21
Hammersmith	33
Hanslick, Eduard	39,75
Haydn, Franz Joseph	31,32,11
Haydn, Mrs. F.J.	31,32
Haydn, Michael	45
Henry VIII, King	7
Herz, Heinrich	19,35
Hexameron	19
Holloway Gaol	23
Holst, R.V.W.	33,34,49
Honegger, Arthur	53,54
Hood, Basil	67
Housman, Alfred Edward	41
Hugo, Victor	63
Hundred Years' War, the	7

I

Ibsen, Henrik	27
Imperial Russian Opera	65
Inquisition, the	73
International Monetary Fund, the	79
Ives, Charles	61

J

Jack the Ripper	55
James II, King	49
Janáček, Leoš	21,22
Java	25
Jeremiah the Prophet	65
Joachim, Josef	15
Jonson, Ben	17
Joplin, Scott	21
Judy	21

K

Khedive of Egypt	71
Kremlin, the	79
Krupp	25,79

L

Lachaise, Père	19
Lanner, Joseph	63

Legrenzi, Guevarra	73	**N**	
Leoncavallo, Ruggiero	47	Napoleon I, Emperor	11,31
Leonore	11,51	Nelson, Admiral Lord	31
Leopold of Tuscany, Grand Duke	77	Neva, River	69
Liszt, Ferenc	35,36,15,19,27	Nijinsky, Albert	65
Longchamps	65	Nordraak, Rickard	27
Lord Chamberlain, the	23	Novello, Ivor	63
Ludwig II, King	75		
Ludwig of Württemberg, Duke	77	**O**	
Lully, Jean Baptiste	37,38,49	Ocarina	17
		Offenbach, Jacques	51,61
		d'Orleans, Madame	37
M		Orlovsky, Count	11
MacDowell, Edward	61		
Maeterlinck, Count Maurice	25		
Magdalenabuch, Anna	9	**P**	
Mahler, Anton	41,42	Pacific 231	21,53,54
Malvern Hills	23	Paris Conservatoire	25
Maria Theresa, Empress	31	Pavlova	65
Marlowe, Christopher	17	Pelleas et Melisande	25
Marshall Aid	55	Pentagon, the	79
Martini, Padre	45	Pepys, Samuel	49
Marxsen, Edward	15	Pillnitz, Electress of	77
Maria Anna Carolina of Saxony,Princess	77	Pirelli, Gian Carlo	73
Mary II, Queen	49	Pius IX, Pope	35
Mascagni, Pietro	47	Pixis, Johann Peter	19
Massenet, Jules	47	Planché, James Robinson	77
Matilda, Waltzing	63	Pony Club, the	23
Mattheson, Johann	29	Poulenc, Francis	53,54
von Meck, Madame	25,69	Priest, Josias	49
Melba, Dame Nellie	51	Private Eye	7
Mendelssohn, Felix	43,44,19,75	Punch, Mr.	21
Mephistopheles	71	Purcell, Henry	49,50
Meyerbeer, Giacomo	75		
Mikado, The	47	**R**	
Milan Conservatoire	71	Rakhmaninov, Sergey	19
Milhaud, Darius	53,54	Raleigh, Sir Water	17
Mimì	19,47	Ramblers' Association, the	11
Moldau, River	21	Rameau, Jean Phillipe	37
Monet, Claude	25	Rasputin, Gregory Efimovich	65
Monkey, Orlando the Marmalade	17,18	Reményi, Eduard	15
Moorfields Cemetery	77	Renoir, Pierre Auguste	25
Mozart, Attrib Leopold	45,46	Rhine, River	59
Mozart, Maria Anna	45,46	Rimbaud, Jean Arthur	25
Mozart, Wolfgang Amadeus	45,46,51,57,69	Rimsky-Korsakov, Nikolay	53,54,45,65,69
Musicians' Union	41	Ripper, Jack the	55
Mussorgsky, Modest	53,54	Robin, Christopher	71

Rome, Prix de	13,25	Sumer is icumen in	7,**8**
Rossini, Gioacchino	51,**52**,45	Sutherland, Duchess of	19
R.S.P.C.A.	79		
Rubinstein, Anton	53	**T**	
Rubinstein, Helena	69	Tailleferre, Germaine	53,**54**
Russell, Ken	23	Tallis, Tom	19
		Tartini, Giuseppe	73
S		Taverner, John	17
Saint-Saëns, Camille	51,69	Teddy Bears' Picnic, the	39,**63**
Salieri, Antonio	45,**57**	Temple, Shirley	59
Sand, George	19	Texier, Rosalie	25
Santa Claus	15	Thalberg, Sigismond	19,**35**
Sardanapalus	13	Torelli, Giuseppe	73
Satie, Erik	53	Transylvania	21
Saxe-Gotha, Duke of	77	Trent, Council of	7
Scala, La	71	Triomphe, l'Arc de	65
Schleswig-Meiningen-Saxe-Strelitz, Duke of	77	Trojans, The	13
Scott, Captain Robert	33	Troldhaugen	27
Scott, Sir Walter	13	Tchaikovsky, Pyotr	69,**70**
Schoenberg, Arnold	55,**56**		
Schubert, Franz	57,**58**	**V**	
Schumann, Clara	15,**59**	Verdi, Giuseppe	71,**72**,47
Schumann, Robert	59,**60**,69	Verlaine, Paul	25
Seven Years' War	29	Victoria, Queen	17,19,**23**
Shakespeare, William	7,**13**,17	Victor Emmanuel, King	71
Sharp, Cecil	33,**53**	Vitus, Saint	21
Skye Boat Song	27	Vivaldi, Antonio	73,**74**
Smetana, Bedřich	21,**22**	Vogl, Michael	57,**58**
Smithson, Harriet	13		
Smyth, Dame Ethel	23,**24**	**W**	
Sousa, John Philip	61,**62**	Wagner, Cosima	35,**75**
Straus, Oscar	63	Wagner, Richard	75,**76**,15,39,51,77
Strauss, Claude Lévi	63	Washington Post, The	61
Struass, Eduard	63	Weber, Carl Maria von	77,**78**
Strauss, Franz	63	Weber, Constanze	45
Strauss, Johann Sebastian I	63	Webern, Anton	55
Strauss, Johann Sebastian II	63,**64**	Wenceslas, King	21
Strauss, Johann Sebastian III	63	Wieck, Clara	59
Strauss, Joseph	63	Wilde, Oscar	67
Strauss, Richard	63,**64**	William III, King	49
Stravinsky, Igor	65,**66**,55	Williams, Ralph Vaughan	31,**33**,34
Strepponi, Guiseppina	71	Wolf, Hugo	15
Sturgis, Julian	67		
Suez Canal	71	**Y**	
Suk, Josef	21	Yale University	21
Sullivan, Sir William	67,**68**		

THE AUTHORS

Howard Burnham, who wrote the words, was born in 1946 in Bournemouth from whence he retired at an early age. Rejected by Eton, King's and the Guards — though not necessarily in that order — he was educated in deepest Dorset and matriculated publicly into the University of Durham where he read History (or rather made it up, which is the same thing).

Graduating in 1968 he worked variously as an actor, museum assistant and car-park attendant while being especially nice to little old ladies with large fixed incomes.

The latter ploy having failed completely, he currently teaches at a girls' prep school in North Yorkshire, for which he writes ripping plays on a wide range of unlikely subjects, from the Boston Tea Party to the Epic of Gilgamesh. In later life he has taken up horn playing, making a meteoric rise to the dizzy heights of Grade V Ass. Bd., but is now stuck on theory. He claims to present a lonely cold exterior and has no cat.

Richard Butterworth, who executed the pictures was born in Dublin in 1932 but makes no great attempt to conceal the fact. After spending most of his early childhood in the fishing village of Dunmore East, County Waterford, he studied at the Winchester College of Art.

He then spent seven years in the design departments of various television companies and now teaches at the same school as the author.

His work has been shown in numerous mixed exhibitions — at Marjorie Parr, Kings Road; The Hendrix Gallery, Dublin; Ewan Phillips, Maddox Street; Austin Hayes, York; and at Duncombe Park, North Yorkshire. Two one-man exhibitions at John Whitley Gallery, Cork Street and The Molesworth Gallery, Dublin were also well received.

Richard Butterworth's singularly interesting paintings are notable for twin elements of mystery and poetry, often overshadowed by a sense of foreboding. He claims not to be able to draw faces, wears size 8½ shoes and has no cat.

EMERSON EDITION is a genuine cottage industry specialising in music for wind instruments. We have published a couple of books before, but these were on subjects related to wind instruments so that the present volume is somewhat of an aberration in more ways than one. Our lovely catalogues are free, although we do appreciate stamps. We have nine ducks, twenty-one chickens and two cats. Please buy this book so we can keep them in the manner to which they are accustomed.